W9-CHM-566

Navaho Blessed BeautyWay Prayer

Great Spirit, may we walk in Beauty.
May Beauty be above us so that we dream of Beauty.
May Beauty be in front of us so that we are led by Beauty.
May Beauty be to the left of us so that we may receive Beauty.
May Beauty be to the right of us so that we may give out Beauty.
May Beauty be behind us so that those who come after us may see Beauty.
May Beauty be inside us so that we might become Beauty.
Great Spirit, may we walk in Beauty.

as taught to Harley SwiftDeer Reagan
by Grandfather Tom Two Bears Wilson,
President of Navaho Native American Church

WOMEN
Of The
LIGHT

The New
SACRED PROSTITUTE

edited by

Kenneth Ray Stubbs, Ph.D.

Secret Garden
Larkspur, California

Published by   Secret Garden
                P.O. Box 67-WCA
                Larkspur, California 94977-0067

Copyright © 1994 by Kenneth Ray Stubbs
            Each individual chapter is co-copyrighted by
            Kenneth Ray Stubbs and its author.
All rights reserved.
Printed in the United States of America.

Cover Painting and Design: Richard Stodart

ISBN 0-939263-12-2

Library of Congress Catalog Card Number: 94-068626

10 9   8   7   6   5   4   3   2   1

Dedicated

to

Barbara Roberts

1922 – 1994

Contents

Introduction

❦

Of the Light

INTRODUCTION:
OF THE LIGHT

by

Kenneth Ray Stubbs, Editor

It just happened to be Halloween night, 1976.

As I walked up the stairs to the artist's loft of a stately San Francisco Victorian in the outlandishly gay Castro district, it was unusually quiet. Outside, Halloween in the Castro, an annually spontaneous local version of a sexual Mardi Gras, had not yet begun.

Inside, I was about to meet Betty Dodson.

Betty had written, self-published, and self-distributed *Liberating Masturbation: A Meditation on Selflove,* a small book dedicated to women. Being outrageous and a fine artist, she had included fifteen of her drawings presenting various shapes, colors, and sizes of female genitalia, or cunts, as she preferred to call them. The book had quickly become an underground bestseller, eventually selling over 150,000 copies before becoming the mainstream hardcover *Sex for One* of today.

In those early days of women's liberation and the feminist movement, Betty was storming the barricades with her book in one hand and a vibrator in the other. Her messages were revolutionary: cunts are beautiful, and women cannot be truly liberated until they take responsibility for their own orgasms.

Betty's book was by a woman, about women, for women. But it was also a book for me, a man who enjoyed being with women. *Liberating Masturbation* was teaching me about variations among women, about a wide range of sexual possibilities. Moreover, in contrast to a fairly common theme of the times, Betty's book did not point a finger of blame at the male gender. Subtly, her words and art invited me also to open up, to grow. Betty celebrated sex and orgasm and sensuality and pleasure and exploration…and I wanted to learn more.

In my late twenties, after teaching music in a Virgin Islands junior high school and sociology in an upstate New York college, I had moved to San Francisco to study Jungian psychology and massage. San Francisco was alive with evolving ideas, avant views on sex, and new experiences integrating the spiritual East and the scientific West.

Attending massage school was to become one of the important decisions in my life. Touch, presence, and connection began to bring me back to my body after spending so many years in my head in academia. Massage became my medium—to relaxation, to meditation, to forgotten pleasures.

Massage is intimate, no matter how therapeutic the technique names may sound, no matter how many sheets drape a client's supposed modesty. In a really good massage, it would be quite possible for either the giver or receiver to experience a variety of basic human feelings, including sexual ones. Yet, in the massage profession, "down there" is regarded as the caste of untouchables. The psychological denial of sexuality and genitals might be far more obvious were it not for the pervasive sexual repression/suppression/oppression throughout our Judeo-Christian cultures.

Sooner or later, doing professional massage, one has to come to terms with sexual energy or burn out and quit the profession. Most just dig their sexual repression trenches deeper. A few quietly choose to include genital massage when they feel it is appropriate. A few feel sexual massage is not for them personally to give but compassionately support the client in finding alternatives.

Eventually, rather than denouncing sexuality, I came to terms with the issue by developing a weekend course in erotic massage for couples: gentle, flowing touch that accepted and nurtured *all* parts of the physical-emotional body.

This was my background I explained to Betty in a phone conversation arranged by a friend who had taken Betty's women's masturbation seminar.

Being a total stranger to Betty, I was surprised when she accepted my invitation to get together to compare notes on my erotic massage seminar and her women's seminar, which as a male I could not attend.

As I walked up the San Francisco Victorian stairs and reflected on her provocative book, I was anticipating meeting an extraordinary person.

From the moment Betty opened the door of the artist's loft, I saw her grounded in her body, both legs planted on the floor. Her voice was earthy; her manner was frank, forward, and self-assured.

Her presence quickly communicated that her sexuality was not a commodity used simply to titillate or to manipulate. Nor was her sexuality to be owned by others. As she had intimated in her writings, sexuality was a path where she was discovering her potential, her wholeness.

On a covered foam pad that served also as a floor bed, we removed our clothing and began our evening of sexual revolution show-and-tell. With massage oil, a few vibrators, and a few other accessories, we demonstrated our genital techniques on each other and ourselves. It was not to become an evening of what most would term *sex*—there just happened not to be any fucking or sucking—but it was very sexual...and more.

What we were really showing each other was far more than technique. We were sharing a knowledge of a way of being, a paradigm where sexuality resides at the center of the sacred circle. Somewhere deep inside, both of us had sensed as youths in the '50s that sex does not equal sin. Yoga, massage, meditation, sex, and orgasm had become our teachers. We had both been learning lessons from the body: our own, our friends' and lovers', and what we had observed from our clients' and students' bodies. That evening we shared our visions.

Near midnight I walked back down the Victorian stairs, out into the carnival. On the Halloween streets there were men dressed in long, golden locks, with watermelon-sized red lips, and glitzy, sequined dresses that even Marilyn would have envied. Through unzipped leather jackets, women bared their breasts and revved up their motorcycle engines, the butchest of vibrators. Hairy buns peeked out of purposefully tattered jeans. All consensual sexual activities and orientations were out of the closet.

Halloween is really a sacred festival time from the Old Religion *Wiccas* (a name sometimes used for a variety of European spiritual traditions predating Christianity). This festival celebrates the sun's transit between the autumnal equinox (equal day and night) and the winter solstice (the shortest day of the year in the Northern Hemisphere). Unable to eradicate the older holy days and nights of often Earth-centered, Goddess-oriented cultures, the patriarchal Church of Rome had to co-opt the celebration, modifying and claiming the festival as one of its own.

There in the Castro that Halloween night, probably very few of the participants considered their earthy festivities a sacred rite. Symbolically, looking back now, I see that evening as a pilgrimage for me. I had visited the archetypal temple priestess as a part of my personal spiritual quest. Having learned from her wisdom in her private chamber, I reentered the temple grounds where a joyous celebration of our primordial pulse—our sexuality—was taking place.

These were my beginning days on a path where my sexuality was a primary catalyst in my spiritual quest. The promise of paradise in the Southern Baptist world of my childhood had became a prison of the soul by my late teens: dogmatic moralities had procreated only shame and guilt...and rebellion with a cause—life *had* to have more meaning than what I had found in church.

In sex and massage I began to find some of that meaning. Then my path crossed those of Betty Dodson and other women and men who were tasting forbidden fruits only to discover that not only is the tree of knowledge available to each individual but that the roots of this tree are firmly planted in the pelvis. As we gained from within ourselves and from one another more knowledge of our sexuality and our spirituality, some of us became somatic teachers, our pedagogy utilizing direct body contact rather than just talking-head verbalism.

Over the centuries the role of sexual teacher/healer/initiator/catalyst has been more often served by women than men. However, as I met more contemporary temple priestesses, I realized that much of what I was doing and teaching was similar to their sacred sexuality practices. (My path has led me to teaching erotic massage and sensate therapy, giving a six-hour sensual pleasuring ceremony, and leading an intensely participatory seminar on Love/Sex/God.) Through meeting these visionaries of sacred sexuality and through my experiences in my own teaching and ceremonial guide roles, I began to realize and appreciate the profound nature of the temple priest/ess, the archetypal sacred prostitute. My purpose in editing and publishing this book is to share my understanding of the women and men dedicated to this service and the role they serve as the *new* sacred prostitute in the modern world.

❦

Women of the Light is primarily a collection of personally written stories by nine women whom over the past two decades I have come to know intimately, sometimes as professional colleague, as student, as teacher, as friend, as lover.

Throughout the centuries and across cultures, they might have been known as *sacred prostitute, temple priestess, sexual healer, sacred whore, Tantrika,* or *FireWoman.* Euphemistically, today they might be called *women of the night*—in a general sense, they all exchange sex for money. For me, they are *women of the light,* not *light* in contrast to *dark* or *black* or *night,* but *light* in contrast to *unaware, unconscious, repression/suppression,* and *denial.*

What makes these friends unique in contemporary times is not that they are compensated for their sexual expression—in some way most of us enter somewhere into the equation of time, attention, affection, security, and other indirect exchanges for sexual connection, marriage being the predominant form in our culture. What makes women of the light unique is that they exchange consciously.

Even more important, they provide a context of compassion and wisdom in the exchange. They are teachers of the heart. They are visionaries, stepping outside of constrictive, traditional beliefs about women and men. Their bodies are their temples, to which they invite others. Their purpose is to support a deeper discovery of the spiritual flame that burns within us all. Sexual energy, in a broad sense, is this flame.

In Paleolithic and Neolithic times, when "God" was more likely to have been female than male, it seems to have been common for women and men to serve in the temples as spiritual-sexual teachers, healers, and priest/esses, at least in European and Middle Eastern areas prior to the rise of Judaism, Christianity, and Islam.

Today women of the light no longer have a public temple where they can share their sacred ceremonies openly. There is no lineage down through which the sacred mysteries can be revealed from high priest/ess to initiate. Legally, socially, and religiously, the sacred prostitute is out in the cold.

Women of the Light is written by seekers who have discovered within themselves, often by trial and error, a sense of the ancient teachings where spirituality fully embraces sexuality, where the heart nurtures the senses. Without the temple, without an unbroken lineage, these women have been pioneers in a reemergence of these ancient teachings and now are becoming the elders, the holders of the wisdom, as most enter their fifties, sixties, and even their seventies.

These women have enriched my life, and I wanted others to know them at least through the printed word. For this book I asked each to write down in her own words a short version of her sexual and spiritual background, experiences, and insights. In most cases, the autobiographical stories remain as originally written with minimal editing. So the reader might have an even broader sense of these unique teachers, I introduce each with some of our personally shared experiences and my vision of some of her contributions.

While each chapter title ("The Porn Star," "The Sex Surrogate," "The Group-Sex Hostess," "The Call Girl," etc.) represents a possible contemporary occupational title, none of these individuals can be reduced to a simplified caption. These pathfinders represent both what we have been and what we can become, sexually and spiritually. Each has risked and stepped outside the common culture and found a more meaningful path that others might also explore.

Touch, the *body*, the *sensual*, the *sexual*, the *spiritual*—these are the common themes throughout all the chapters, for these temple priestesses are *embodiments* of profound teachings. Beyond these themes, the stories present a wide spectrum of human sexual experiences—their sexual lives are far from the ordinary. To the extent that we have repressed our sexual feelings and expressions, we may find reading about these lifestyles to be challenging, possibly deeply confronting.

My hope is that these personal accounts will open doors of understanding. These women of the light have chosen a different path than most and have discovered a wisdom available to us all. Their lives, if we are willing, can shed light on our own.

JULIET CARR

❦

THE PORN STAR

Introduction to

JULIET CARR

The first time I met Juliet was in a bathtub.

At the time, I knew her as Juliet Carr rather than by her screen and stage name, Juliet Anderson. Juliet had become very popular as the adventurous character Aunt Peg in a number of sexually explicit films.

Knowing only that she was a porn star, I was curious when Juliet phoned to arrange a time to receive the Secret Garden Ceremony. Juliet had heard about this six-hour sensual ceremony from a mutual friend who was an actress in a pilot film depicting sexual fantasies more typically expressed by some women. After filming a long close-up of a man's hands gently caressing the whole length of a woman's nude body, Juliet, the film's director, remarked how she would love to have something like that scene happen in her real life. Our mutual friend responded with a description of the Secret Garden Ceremony she had received a few years earlier.

First, in a guided meditation with her physical body reclining on a bed, she had been led into an imaginary meadow. There she was invited to see with her inner eyes all the colors in the meadow, to feel on her bare feet the texture of the earth as she walked across the meadow, to listen to the winds, to feel their caress, to step into a stream passing through the meadow, to float and to flow down-stream, to surrender and become one with the water. As she drifted downstream, a voice chanted a melody, encouraging her to let go and simply *be.*

After a timeless time, the voice invited her consciousness to come back to the physical world, to open her eyes, rise slowly, and accom-pany the two men, robed in kimonos, standing beside her. As the three entered the bathroom, she saw a single candle lighting the bubbled bath waters. A fragrance of almost recognizable herbs filled the mists.

After disrobing and entering the warm waters, she rested her head on an air pillow as the two ceremonial guides presented a plat-ter of ripe, sliced fruits with whipped cream. Meditative music in the background blended with the tastes and the fragrances and the warm glow of the candlelight. She and the two men were nude. They were strangers becoming lovers, though lovers of a different kind, dancing in the realm of the senses.

Following the feeding, she began to merge with the bath wa-ters, this time physically, as four hands bathed her with peppermint soap and loofahs, and rinsed her with sponges. To complete the bath, a voice from one of the ceremonial guides asked her to slowly slide forward so he could slip in behind her. Leaning back in his arms, she could hear, embraced, with her eyes closed, the airy notes of a silver flute played by the other guide. Together, the stillness of the water, the warmth of the embrace, and the sound waves from the flute wove an encompassing sphere, a space outside of time and place. She went inside…inside to the inner, secret garden.

Afterward she was dried and led to a massage table, where for the next hour the four hands massaged her with feathers, furry mittens, and fragrant oil. Finally, she was tucked into bed and read a bedtime story. It ended with the words *fly free across forever*.

This was the experience our mutual friend described to Juliet. The Secret Garden Ceremony, a journey that nurtured the senses, was available for a fee. No sex was expected in exchange; neither were the ceremonial guides likely to be sexually available.

It fit Juliet's fantasy. For her personally, though, she requested that her ceremonial guides be a female and a male. As the co-originator of the Secret Garden Ceremony, this is how I came to meet in a bathtub—and appreciate—Juliet Carr.

In such an intimate ceremony, where the recipient is invited to entrust her body, her psyche, and her heart to two strangers, though it be for only a few hours, she is revealed. Facades become veils through which a deeper self is seen. Juliet describes herself as a born ham. In her Secret Garden Ceremony what I first saw was the "onstage" persona; beneath was an immensely inquisitive spirit, with a childlike wonder, ready to discover the next step. This natural curiosity is one of her most valuable strengths, what has guided her to solutions to deal with physical pain from an almost lifelong illness.

After her ceremony I began to realize the benefits to Juliet in being a born ham. In a culture where sexuality is both segregated to repressed ghettos in the mind and at the same time superficially glorified with tinsel, Juliet's "onstage" persona has enabled her to become a temple priestess, a sacred prostitute, in a modern, technological world. Not unlike Greta Garbo and Marilyn Monroe, though in a different genre, Juliet became a star because of what her image evoked in the viewers watching the silver screen.

In the thought-provoking book entitled *The Sacred Prostitute*, Nancy Qualls-Corbett, Ph.D., presents us with an understanding of a concept that embraces the spirit and the flesh: the sacred prostitute is a human being who embodies the goddess of love. In various ancient cultures, there were temples devoted to the worship of the goddess of love, Aphrodite and Venus being the most well known in the modern Western world. In these temples, where sex was a sacrament and ecstasy a divinely inspired state, the priestesses often were sacred prostitutes. In a physical body, they were revered as the Goddess's emissaries, the revealers and the holders of the sacred truths, and sometimes the incarnation of the Goddess herself. Sexuality was celebrated publicly, joyously, sacredly, with the sacred prostitute being guide, teacher, healer, transformer, catalyst.

Today the earthy goddess of love and sexuality has been displaced by a sky god wrathfully punishing those who partake—too much—in the pleasures of the flesh. The contemporary predominant religions emphasize the masculine in the sacred domain, but the deep psychological need for the sacred feminine remains. She—the archetype of the sacred feminine, the Goddess, the goddess of love—still lives, though through avenues deemed secular and sometimes crassly commercial: When there is no room in the religious inn, where else can the human psyche turn to give birth to a sacred child? Today the sacred-feminine archetype finds expression through the images of the Garbos and the Marilyns and more recently the Madonnas and the porn stars like Juliet, who have become the new temple priestesses, their images projected onto the temple walls of the movie theaters and the television screens where millions of devotees pay tribute, enthralled when somewhere inside a chord has resonated with the larger-than-life, feminine love/sex symbol.

Juliet became a porn star in her forties, guided quite unexpectedly into the genre by Spirit, her term for God/dess. She personally enjoyed sex immensely, and though she felt the porn plots superficial, she discovered the films to be a new playground, an arena where she could be on stage and express her creativity. She could be a teacher encouraging her male and female viewers to expand their sensual and sexual horizons, to awaken to the deeper meanings that sex had brought to her own life.

Juliet's sex career has spanned from screen, stage, and phone sex to giving and teaching erotic massage. After her Secret Garden Ceremony, as I came to know more of Juliet's life, I found that she genuinely cares for her viewers, fans, and clients. Though holding a different belief than mainstream religion, Juliet is a missionary. Sexuality has been a liberation for her, and she has a message to teach: Sex is good, sex is holy.

THE PORN STAR

by

Juliet Carr

He reclines, nude, on his back, on a slightly raised futon as I gently stroke his body from head to toe, alternating feather-light touch with my hands, nails, fingertips, lips, tongue, hair, arms, breasts, and full-body nude contact. His skin ripples with "orgabumps" as the orgasmic energy intensifies. "Oh yes," he sighs, "it feels so good!" Seeing his erect cock, he gasps, "Oh, my God…it hasn't been this hard in years!" I smile and continue to caress his ears, elbows, feet, and every inch in-between. I tell him it's OK to surrender to the delicious erotic sensations, to feel instead of think, to breathe deeply, and to let the energy slowly spread out from his genitals to his entire body. I ask him to turn on his side into a fetal position and hug the pillow. I am now able to increase the orgasmic energy by repeatedly stroking from his buttocks up his spine and down his back, arms, and legs. When he turns onto his back again, I ask him to touch me so that our sexual energies can merge. He quivers in an intense orgasm. "Don't hold your breath," I remind him. "Feel the release all the way from the top of your head to your fingertips and toes." My hands gently and slowly continue their caresses....

Afterward, we lie in each other's arms, cherishing the deep connection we've made. This is Bill's first visit, and he is understandably overcome with emotion—unable to hide tears of joy and a smile reminiscent of a happy five-year-old boy. From our previsit telephone conversation I know that he and his wife of thirty-two years haven't been sexual for the last ten. They don't even touch anymore. He hadn't been sexual with anyone since his marriage and had mixed feelings about coming to see me. Now Bill confides that his cock has been limp for many years—even on the rare occasions he masturbates—and that his main purpose in seeking me out was to find out if he was impotent. We share a laugh at the fun we've had banishing his greatest fear. Along the way, he has also learned that his nipples, ears, and ankles are sensitive and a real turn-on when stimulated, and that orgasm is more than genital release. Since it is a one-and-a-half-hour appointment, he gets onto the massage table, where I give him an excellent therapeutic massage. I tell him that on his next visit I will show him some touching techniques...that he can practice on me.

Before Bill leaves I give him homework (I prefer *homepleasuring*): (1) masturbate daily to learn to delay ejaculation while riding the waves of orgasmic energy moving through his entire body, (2)

experiment with different types of stimulation on nongenital erogenous areas, (3) initiate nonsexual, gentle touch with his wife. We
part with a hug. "It's incredible to realize, Juliet, that your gifts would
brand you a witch, a slut, a whore in much of the world today. To
me you're an angel. I can't thank you enough."

Bill was, indeed, a happy man. Touching his wife gently, sensually, but nonsexually eventually aroused her passion, and their sex
life became fulfilling. That was five years ago. Bill continues to visit
me because what I offer fuels *their* flame—positively affecting not
only their marriage but the quality of their lives in general.

How did I get into this unusual profession? I didn't wake up
one morning a sexual healer/catalyst. The easiest answer is that I
retired from being an X-rated film and stage actress and needed another venue for my sexual creativity.

At age forty I answered an ad in the *San Francisco Chronicle*:
"Attractive woman over 18 wanted for soft-core sex show. Lots of
fun, short hours, good pay." A few months earlier I had moved
to this city from six and a half years in Finland. I had not intended to
return to the USA, but Spirit directed me to "return home and begin
working on myself." Since my early twenties I had been aware that
I was guided by Spirit, which goes by many names: God, Goddess,
wisdom, the Divine, higher consciousness, intuition. I knew from
experience to be attentive, to listen, to follow. I had no idea what the
directive meant, but I knew I would eventually find out.

I specifically chose the San Francisco Bay Area because of its
reputation as Mecca for independent filmmakers. I had been a very
successful radio program producer of programs in English about
Finland that were distributed worldwide. I wanted to go from painting verbal pictures to filming documentaries. Patience not being one
of my virtues, I was in despair of ever finding out what I was supposed to do next with my life. I was suffering from culture shock,
depression, lack of money and a job, poor health, and horniness when

I answered the ad, hoping for a little excitement, money, and *sex*! Until then my health and happiness had mainly depended on sexual satisfaction. In San Francisco I couldn't get laid no matter how I tried. I had been ignorant of the large gay population and the scarcity of available heterosexual men before moving here. My well-being was at stake. I had to do something—quick!

Amazingly, I was hired for the show (providing I not reveal my age to the boss). Even more surprising, the very next day I was offered a role in a big-budget, high-quality, X-rated film, *Pretty Peaches* by Alex d'Renzy. I intended it to be a one-time fling, but my Inner Voice told me this was to be my new path. Me, a porno actress? Never in a million years would I have guessed it. It was not how I had envisioned being involved in the film business. But I knew better than to question Spirit, so I swallowed my fears and embarked on my new career. I was in numerous 8 and 16 mm loops, 35 mm films, and videos. In some I had a bit part; in others I was the star. What set me apart from most other women in the business was my age, my erotic imagination, and my genuine love of sex. I was a mature, good-looking, sophisticated woman who gloried in her lust. I realized that pornography was about fantasies, not to be taken seriously, so I developed a style that combined sex with comedy. I had no guidelines, acting lessons, or even rehearsals, so I just did what came naturally. I saved many a production with humor and improvisation. The scripts were so lame it was embarrassing. Since the stories weren't meant to be believable, I did my best to at least make them entertaining…and most important, to enjoy myself. Women were also my fans—for at last they had someone they could identify with. I quickly went from porno actress to "Sex Goddess," a title bestowed on me by others. It seems that I had captured an audience that was ready for an archetypal goddess of passionate sex.

We made so little money in those days (a few hundred dollars per film and no residuals) that we all had to have other sources of income. I took menial jobs behind the camera, wrote and posed for the "skin magazines," was on television and radio talk shows, gave lectures, did phone sex, formed a production company, and produced and directed several X-rated videos. As soon as I was well known, I created stage shows which I took on the road. It was in theater that I excelled. I was not the type to be a lap dancer or circuit stripper. I was an actress, so I created a one-woman show with a cast of characters: "Helen, the Housewife," "Cassie, the Cook," "Nurse Naughty," "Elaine, the Executive" and many more—women who beneath their facades of respectability were wanton and proud of it. After a skit I would talk with the audience: answer questions, dispel sexual myths, give useful advice on how sensuality and sexuality can improve the quality of life, and was self-revealing about my own journey and struggles to wholeness through the integration of mind, body, and spirit. The final part of my show was a Polaroid photo session in the lobby. Before each picture I gave the person, usually a man, a loving hug. For countless men, it was the first time in many years they had held a woman in their arms. The experience never failed to be profound for both of us.

During these years I was attending a number of workshops on personal growth, massage, and sacred sexuality, all of which greatly influenced my current work. I also deepened my spiritual practice through meditation and prayer.

After seven years I knew it was time to quit the adult entertainment business. I moved to a small town in the mountains and went inward to ask for guidance for what I was to do next. While I waited for an answer, I managed a bed-and-breakfast inn, cleaned houses, cooked and cared for children, went to therapeutic massage school, and bought a home. After five years of voluntarily abstaining from sex to replenish my sexual fires, I was ready for a lover and started looking for a personal relationship. I didn't give a thought to professional sex. Much to my surprise, after a few months of giving strictly what nonsexual massage therapists call "therapeutic" massage, the desire to incorporate the erotic arose quite naturally. Since I couldn't do it in the conservative town in which I lived, one week per month I went to Oakland where I practiced the art of sexual healing through touch. Eventually the commute and living a double life became a burden, and I moved permanently to the Bay Area, where I now live.

Because my work is very emotionally and physically demanding, I see a maximum of twenty-three clients a month. I must be alert, rested, sensitive, centered, and maintain my psychic boundaries so that I am not drained by clients' imbalances. This is difficult to do! I spend a lot of time alone frequently going to my home in the mountains to replenish myself. I wrote this chapter at the edge of a serene, alpine lake. Quiet, beauty, and nature soothe my soul and release my creativity.

Shortly before I moved back to the city, I had a hysterectomy in which both ovaries were (unnecessarily) removed. What a shock to discover that after the operation my libido had disappeared. I was faced with the challenge of finding new ways to get turned on and to orgasm. I recalled the pleasant tingling I'd felt in my youth when my skin was lightly raked with fingertips and nails. I expanded that concept and added it to my erotic repertory. My clients and I were soon having mutual, full-body, nonintercourse, multiple orgasms. Wow!

 Most of my clients are married, thirty-five- to eighty-year-old men who need nurturing more than sexual release, although they rarely admit it. They answer my occasional ad in *The Spectator: A Sex Newsmagazine*, published in Berkeley, California. All economic and ethnic groups seek me out.

The session with Bill is a typical one with older men. Younger men come to me for different reasons. If they are married, usually they love their wives and children, and describe their marriages as happy. But with their spouses also employed full-time outside the home, intimate time together is infrequent and their sexual desires are not met with their wives. Men are used to paying for pleasure and don't hesitate to peruse ads for these services. The men I see want a woman who not only is comfortable with her sexuality but celebrates it: a mature, caring woman who will uninhibitedly give and receive tender, loving touch; who will listen to, encourage, and validate their sexuality. Often I am a man's only confidante. It is well documented that men go to prostitutes mainly to be touched and listened to. Ironically, by merely offering intercourse, high-class prostitutes get paid double and more than what I charge even if they only give the client a "handjob." Why then don't I have intercourse? It's a health, not a moral, issue. It's not safe sex (even with condoms, from my perspective), and it's not how I am to share my body with clients.

Lately I have been getting a few women clients. Some are married; others are single or divorced, They are twenty to forty years of age, Caucasian, and middle-class. All are brave and curious about their sexuality. They come to me from my workshops or lectures or are referred by therapists. Occasionally, a husband or partner will share where he has acquired his improved lovemaking and communication skills and why he has become easier to get along with. Instead of being threatened, some of the women partners come to me to learn more about their own erotic natures: how, when, and where they like to be touched; what is sexually exciting; how to communicate their desires. For some women, their entire bodies are erotic and what turns them on is more varied than many men would suspect. I also show women different ways to pleasure a partner.

Most important, I emphasize women's right to full sexual lives of their own design. To even admit being interested in sex is a primary taboo for most women. What about her lust…fantasies…sexual deprivation…fears? To get what she wants is a taboo that must be challenged.

Occasionally I get couple clients. Tony and Anita offer a good example of the benefits of experiential, sensual/sexual couple counseling. They had a twenty-year friendship and a ten-year marriage that was in danger of dissolution. They had been childhood playmates, then high-school sweethearts who married after graduation. Slowly their marriage grew stale, communication broke down, sex became predictable and infrequent. Tony has a vivid erotic imagination. Anita has a more practical nature. He compensated for his unhappiness by overeating, she by overworking. When food failed to fill the void, he looked for a play partner in *The Spectator*. I interviewed him in depth before setting up an appointment. After three visits the change in Tony was so noticeable that Anita asked him what was going on. He took a chance and told her about me. Not only was she totally understanding but asked him if I also saw couples. Anita and I had a long talk on the phone, during which I explained that she needed to have at least two sessions alone with me. After that, they could see me together if they so desired. That is what they did, and their relationship thrived. We have also become friends over the years. Every once in a while Anita tells Tony he needs a "Juliet fix," and he gladly obliges. He maximizes the adventure, first by making the appointment far enough in advance to extend the titillation of anticipation, second by engaging himself totally in our session, and third by basking in the afterglow and sharing it with Anita for weeks afterward. Sometimes Anita comes to see me alone for TLT (tender, loving touch).

❦

Being in the second half century of my life, I can see some other major forces that shaped who I am today. Most important, I got a good start: conceived in love and raised in a loving and affectionate family. My father was a talented musician, a jazz trumpet player with the big bands and Hollywood studio orchestras in the '30s and '40s. As the first Pinkey Tomlin "band baby," I also got lots of attention and affection from the forty-odd musicians and their wives and girlfriends. From the time I could walk and talk, I was singing and dancing—a natural performer who never hesitated when asked to entertain my family and parents' friends. I was a born ham! At age three I already knew I wanted to be an actress. My parents, knowing firsthand the unsavory aspects of show business, were not about to let *their* daughter be exposed to its perils. I was furious and acted out my anger with high drama. Eventually I found other artistic outlets: drawing, painting, writing, and playing the piano.

When I was ten years old, I became very ill with a variety of mysterious ailments. For the next eight years, I was in constant, often excruciating pain, frequently in hospitals for tests or surgeries. While my peers were enjoying school, sports, and parties, I was bedridden. I attended school sporadically, excelled academically, but had no close friends and was physically awkward. My one constant companion was pain.

I'm eternally grateful to my parents and sister during these difficult years for their unconditional love and lots of tender, loving touch. As a family we had always scratched or lightly stroked one another's backs, heads, faces, and arms. For me it became an antidote to pain. From this experience I learned to associate loving touch with healing.

An unfortunate discovery I made was that being ill got me the attention I craved. My bed became a stage, and I perfected the role of the tragic heroine, my imagination fueled by books, dreams, and radio theater. What saved my life was my strong will to conquer my afflictions. When I overheard doctors say that I probably wouldn't survive an operation or at best I would be a cripple, I was determined to prove them wrong. And I did! But not until I went away to college and no longer had to follow the dictates of doctors or my parents did I begin to get well. I took charge of my life and sought out alternative approaches to health, such as yoga, macrobiotics, acupuncture, herbs, and meditation. After an initial adjustment period, the change in me was remarkable. Soon I was backpacking, dancing, eating formerly forbidden foods—and feeling better than I ever had. I still experienced pain, but it was manageable.

When I went to college, in those days a girl went to find a husband not pursue a career. In addition to warning me of the evils of the entertainment business, my parents implored me to become neither an artist (it would undoubtedly bring me poverty and disrespect) nor a teacher (which would doom me to spinsterdom). So naturally I chose a major in art and a minor in English—intending to teach both. The "good girl" rebelled! And then there was *sex*! But this was the '50s, and nice girls didn't do *it* until marriage. But already at seventeen I knew marriage and children weren't part of my plans. After so many years of confinement and acquiescence, I craved freedom and independence. I was curious about the societal preoccupation with sex, so I decided to find out about all the hoopla. I methodically orchestrated the loss of my virginity by being fitted for a diaphragm, choosing the man, and promising intercourse if we could first spend the summer kissing and exploring each other's bodies. My parents had given me some sex education, but up until age twenty I had never "played doctor," kissed a boy, or dated. I'd not even had the desire to masturbate because my abdominal/genital area had always been a source of pain.

The summer of '58 was fun. And true to my word, the night before my first lover returned to a distant college, we "went all the way." This was a momentous occasion for reasons besides getting virginity out of the way. Specifically, through intercourse with my lover, for the first time in my life, I felt shivers of pleasure coursing through my whole body. Wow! He rolled over and went to sleep, while I lay awake savoring the implications of my discovery. Later I learned that endorphins, natural pain inhibitors, are released during good sex. At that moment, however, all I cared about was that I floated free of pain. I was astonished, ecstatic, and an immediate convert to the healing aspects of guilt-free sex. Lust had liberated me from the torments of chronic pain. I didn't care if parents, church, or society disapproved, sexual passion would be my "drug of choice." I wasted no time seeking out men who weren't intimidated by my assertiveness, intelligence, and lust, and who were willing to pleasure me the way *I* liked—and I didn't hesitate to show them how. Thus began my lifelong search for wholeness through the integration of mind and body, spirituality and sexuality.

It wasn't until 1992 that I finally found out the cause of my lifelong health problems. I have two genetic diseases: manic-depression and Crohn's disease (an inflammatory bowel disease). Both are incurable but treatable. Knowing this helps explain my years of abdominal distress, mood swings, hysterics, and breakdowns. Nowadays, I use Western, Chinese, and East Indian Ayurvedic healing systems to keep both illnesses under control.

When I was twenty-one, I was lucky enough to meet a randy young sailor with a heart of gold, the body of an Adonis, and a cock of steel, who agreed to teach me all the things he had learned in the numerous whorehouses he'd visited around the world. He was a gentle, loving teacher; I was an eager, passionate pupil. If sex was going to play a crucial role in my life, I wanted to be good at it! We were friends as well as lovers and still keep in touch by mail after all these years.

For the next thirty years I had numerous relationships with men in many countries. Not only did we share adventures and great sex, but my partners, not just I, became more balanced and healthier. I was onto something else—not yet aware, however, of its significance.

Not surprisingly, there was a conflict between my attitude and that of Christianity regarding sex. When we were teenagers, my sister and I attended the Burbank Presbyterian Church. Every Sunday our parents, who were atheists, stayed home and made love while we went to church. It was the first place I felt accepted. I sang in the choir, taught Sunday School, joined the Youth Group, and chose to be baptized at age sixteen. It was during this time I felt that God had special plans for me or "He" wouldn't let me suffer years of illness. But then I got into trouble for questioning the accuracy of the Bible, as well as the discrepancies between parishioners' piety on Sunday and their unchristian words and deeds the rest of the week, and other puzzling inconsistencies. I was reprimanded and told I lacked faith. Needing to be liked and to belong to a group, I shut up and was obedient—until I discovered sex. I inquired of several denominations and they all said sex outside marriage was a sin—no exceptions. This radically changed my attitude about Christianity. I just knew that anything that felt so good and had the power to heal was right and holy. I had no trouble choosing between Christianity and Sex. After an initial period of agnosticism, I explored other philosophies and religions throughout the world. I may have given up the Church, but not my belief in the Divine. Nowadays, I observe the seasonal changes with Native American rituals and Goddess rituals with women's groups. My meditation practice is from the Theravada Buddhist tradition called Vipassana, or Insight Meditation.

I am frequently asked why I haven't pursued a higher degree than a B.A. Why didn't I become a marriage, family, and child counselor or a sexologist? I purposely chose not to take the academic route, because I would be unable to touch my clients without risk of having my license revoked. I am a teacher, but I can only teach what I know from sensate experience, which includes sensual touch. I use my body as a *laboratory* and pass on what I learn—about diet, exercise, sex, spirituality.

There are many kinds of hands-on healing. What characterizes my work is I was born with a gift of tender, loving touch and I teach that sacred sexuality is a means to health. I regard the body as the temple of the soul. We must give the body healthy food, exercise, relaxation, and good sex. If we neglect our bodies, we live fragmented lives. To honor the body requires that we honor our sexuality. But there are few safe outlets for exploration in this area. By creating a conscious and sacred space and by establishing emotional and physical boundaries for us both, I offer people the opportunity to explore their sensuality, to be vulnerable, and to be lovingly accepted as sexual beings. As long as the sessions are *mutually* enjoyable and positively affect both of our lives, we will continue our "erotic dance." Most of my clients see me regularly—for up to eight years.

I have tried other, more socially acceptable professions, but I have always gravitated back into the sexual arena. For years I wondered why I was given this role. I now realize that being a sexual healer/catalyst is a blessing. By guiding others on their journeys to wholeness by honoring their erotic natures, I am able to maintain my own health and happiness.

When I am asked what my profession is, I create a title to suit the circumstances: mind/bodywork facilitator, therapist, teacher, relationship counselor. These satisfy the superficially interested. Nowadays, *sex educator* is socially acceptable and garners few requests for details. When I feel safe, I openly admit to being a "sacred erotic artist" and offer details if asked. I regard myself as catalyst, a visionary, a sexual healer, a sacred intimate. I deeply believe in my work and am committed to being a guide for those who seek connection with the Divine through their sexuality.

How others view me depends on who they are. To other sex professionals I am a colleague, to sacred-erotic goddesses I am a sister, to religious radicals I am a whore, to the "establishment" I am a dilemma, to porn fans I am a sex queen, to some of my clients I am a saint, to different members of my birth family I am everything from an embarrassment to a great role model whom they love because of or in spite of my lifestyle. I keep a low profile at home so my neighbors probably think of me as a middle-aged massage therapist and counselor who likes children and animals, works in her yard, recycles, often wears baggy clothes and no makeup, drives an old car, and lives a quiet, simple life with her partner, their two cats, lots of books, and no TV.

I doubt I could do my work without the unconditional love and support of my partner, Charles. We have been together since 1989 and both see this relationship as lifelong. We met when he came to see me as a client, so he is intimately acquainted with what I do. He admires my gifts, respects my work, is patient with my difficult temperament. He is my anchor, my safe harbor in the storm. Our relationship is based on friendship and love, not on sex. He holds me when I cry and is learning to stand his ground when I get bossy. So what if he hates vegetables and exercise, wears mismatched clothes, and likes cowboy music—obviously if he weren't an eccentric, we wouldn't be together.

Mine is not an easy life. I must be discreet and circumspect—careful in whom I confide. I would like to be able to take my work outside the Bay Area, and I wish I could share my gifts with more women, to help empower them in their sexuality. It helps me to remember that throughout history, visionaries often have been vilified by the majority. My heroes and heroines have been those who rocked the boat.

One of the most important validations came from the late Rev. Carol Knox, minister of a local Unity Church. During my years in the adult entertainment industry, she commended me for doing "missionary work"—by stressing the importance of not splitting spirituality from sexuality, by reaching people who would never go to church or to a therapist, and especially by living what I taught.

When I first added the sexual dimension to my massage work in 1987, I was concerned whether or not it was "right livelihood," so I consulted with one of the most respected Vipassana teachers in this country. He asked me where the impetus came from. I replied without hesitation, "My heart."

He put my concerns to rest. "Spirit works in many ways," he said. "Be grateful for your gifts, and use them wisely."

BARBARA ROBERTS

❧

THE SEX SURROGATE

Introduction to

Barbara Roberts

I first heard of Barbara Roberts from her daughter, who was leading a meditative sexuality seminar. Barbara's name continued to come up in conversations with fellow sexologists, the term for people who academically study the interdisciplinary field of human sexuality. Barbara had become one of the first sex surrogates in California. She had also established at her Los Angeles sex therapy center a training program for other women and men who wanted to become professionals in this innovative, if not revolutionary, approach to sexual dysfunctions.

While the Secret Garden Ceremony was never intended as a therapeutic process nor does it focus on sexual functioning, there are several similarities with sex surrogacy. As an opportunity to meet one of my hero/ines, I offered Barbara a gift of the ceremony, and she accepted.

Barbara would probably not fit anyone's expectations of a sex pioneer. A nun—that could easily be a first impression seeing her on the street. Outwardly she is both unassuming and unobtrusive. Conservative, almost nondescript, often characterizes her clothing. Any makeup there might be is barely noticeable. Her voice is soft; her manner, quiet though purposeful. Her subtle smile emanates, suggesting an inner peace and inner knowing.

In a sense, Barbara *is* a nun. I think of her as a bodhisattva, the Buddhist name for an enlightened being who chooses to remain in the continuing cycle of death and rebirth until all sentient beings become enlightened and can leave the cycle together. In her mid-sixties Barbara had several intense energetic sexual experiences that led her to search much more deeply into her spiritual nature, a path she had already been exploring for many years. She consequently retired from her active practice as a sex therapist, sex surrogate, and founder/director of the Center for Social and Sensory Learning in order to devote more time to her spiritual quest, eventually studying closely with a Buddhist monk. Even now in her seventies—the eldest of the women of the light writing in this book—Barbara teaches to her fellow retirement home residents a weekly "personal explorations" class on "mindfulness in living and in dying."

Barbara Roberts is also a rebel with a cause; her conscience has led her far outside society's ways. She was active in civil rights activities in high school before World War II, and during her college days served as a union organizer. A 1946 graduate of the nontraditional Antioch College and a licensed social worker living in Pennsylvania, she discovered nudism and, as she says, "drug my husband and children off to a join a nudist camp." She was involved in the early days of the women's movement. When she learned of the counterculture developing on the West Coast, she pulled up stakes from her psychotherapy practice in Philadelphia and headed to California. There, as a sex therapist, she attended Masters and Johnson's first training in sex surrogacy.

Before William Masters, M.D., and Virginia Johnson's publication of *Human Sexual Response* in 1966 and *Human Sexual Inadequacy* in 1970, most sex therapy was basically a lengthy verbal/mental process in the psychotherapist's office, often talking about childhood traumas. Sex is somatic, but the therapeutic process touched only the psyche.

Masters and Johnson brought the body back to sex, at least to sex therapy. They made two significant contributions: *sensate focus exercises* and *sex surrogates*, two rather clinical terms for some rather simple concepts. *Sensate focus* means to focus on sensations, to be consciously aware of the sensory experiences occurring in the body. In sensual/sexual actions we often get so caught up in our expectations, our comparisons with the past, our passions in the moment that we become unconscious of the moment. In our ravenous consumption, we miss the subtle, sweet nectar. Sensate focus exercises are designed to help couples experience more fully and more profoundly the sensations that are already there in lovemaking.

But what if you do not have a sexual partner? This is where the function of the sex surrogate comes in. Masters and Johnson, because they were in the medical field, were able to legitimize the use of sex surrogates. Writing for other psychological and medical clinicians, they selected for the new profession a title that I feel leaves a lot to be desired. A sex surrogate is by no means merely a *substitute* set of genitals. *Educator, ceremonial guide,* and *catalyst* give a more complete connotation.

The standard procedure is for a client with a sexual dysfunction to begin therapy with a sex therapist. Then, if a sex surrogate is needed, the therapist selects an appropriate surrogate. The client has some sessions with the surrogate only, some with the therapist only, and some with both.

Sex surrogates are unique within the field of sex therapy because they use their body directly, physically, intimately, with the client. Teaching how to give and receive sensitive touch, developing social and communication skills, always role modeling the concepts of nonperformance and nondemand, and when therapeutically appropriate, having manual, oral, or genital sex with the client—these are the sometimes essential functions a therapist cannot, will not, or does not know how to do.

As a sex therapist, Barbara felt she could not know how to utilize fully a sex surrogate unless she herself had experienced the role firsthand. So, again being a rebel with a cause, she chose to be trained as a surrogate, a rather uncommon occurrence for a therapist. Moreover, since Masters and Johnson provided surrogate-assisted therapy for heterosexual male clients only, it remained for other pioneers such as Barbara to train and use surrogates for heterosexual and lesbian women and gay men.

In the modern world, sex surrogacy is the most legitimized of the roles available to today's temple priestess. The temple, however, must now be disguised as a psychological or medical clinic. Now a worshipper must have a pathological condition; a sexual disorder classification is the temple entrance requirement. The psychotherapist and medical doctor have become the new high priest/ess. And because a sex surrogate usually works under the auspices of the therapist or doctor, the new sacred prostitute is given legal and social sanctuary.

Barbara is keenly aware that working within a pathological framework has severe limitations. At the same time she knows sex therapy and surrogacy serve an immensely valuable healing function for many members of society. In personal conversations she expressed she has "felt led" to step outside the mainstream in order to serve others in the mainstream.

Barbara Roberts has ventured in her seventy years where others fear censure. While risking societal disapproval, she has been able to remain centered and grounded. Her quiet but determined nature has opened doors for others. Her courage to be free is a model for us all.

THE SEX SURROGATE

by

Barbara Roberts

Jay was divorced. He'd been dating but hadn't found anyone with whom he wanted to spend a lot of time. He'd had sex with some of the women he'd dated but found it not very satisfying. In fact, he was having trouble with coming too fast. Sometimes he came just at the point of penetration. This was extremely embarrassing. Especially with the women he liked the best, the ones who were pretty and sexy, he had the most trouble. He'd decided to find out if sex therapy would help.

When Jay and I first talked, he told me that he was divorced and had settled on living the rest of his life as a bachelor. He wasn't interested in getting married again, but he did want to have a normal and satisfying sex life. All he wanted was to learn how to hold back his ejaculation long enough for both him and a partner to come to orgasm. He asked me if there was any solution to his problem. I told Jay that there definitely was but that he would need to have a partner to practice with. Jay said that he didn't know anyone he would feel comfortable asking to do that. It was too embarrassing. I asked what he thought about working with a surrogate partner.

Jay knew that I used surrogate partners to assist with the sex therapy—that's why he had chosen me as a therapist—but he had many questions. What if he wasn't turned on to the surrogate? Since she was the expert, if he learned how to perform with her, how could he be sure that he would be able to function with other women?

I told Jay that, from my experience, if he learned the things he needed to learn with a surrogate, it was almost guaranteed that he could do the same later with partners of his choice. I explained that he would learn the magic wasn't in the surrogate but within himself. One of the causes of sexual problems is the belief that it's the other person who is responsible for one's turn-on and satisfaction. At first he would just have to take my word for that and find out for himself as the therapy progressed.

I matched Jay with Ann, an experienced surrogate who was a couple of years older than he, attractive but not what society would call a raving beauty. Jay wasn't thrilled with my choice but agreed to give it a try. During the feedback times with me after Jay and Ann had been alone doing touching exercises, Ann had to do most of the talking. She said that Jay followed my instructions very closely but that he didn't share much of how he was feeling about it all. Nor could I get him to talk about it. All he would say was that it was OK. He seemed to be unusually reticent.

Ann, on the other hand, told me and Jay how much she enjoyed his touch and how comfortable she felt with him but that she wished he would share some of his feelings with her. She was feeling "left out" and didn't know if he enjoyed himself, even a little bit. I too wondered what was behind his silent facade.

During a subsequent session, Ann and Jay ended early, urgently wanting to talk with me. Ann had been giving Jay a face caress, silently and slowly exploring every line and contour. Suddenly Jay grasped her hands with his as he tried to choke back the tears that were welling up in his eyes. In that moment Jay realized that what he really wanted was a close, intimate relationship with a woman, not just the ability to perform sexually. He had felt a tenderness and involvement with Ann, which he had not thought possible. After all, she was only his surrogate, someone he would never see again when the therapy sessions ended. Now, at last, Jay was beginning to believe that Ann really did care for him. The fact that she was not his ideal type just seemed to fade away.

Ann told Jay that she was relieved and complimented that he had finally shared some of his inner self with her. She explained that, yes, she did care for him and wanted him to be able to live his dreams. And, equally important, she was able to thoroughly enjoy the touching exercises because not only did his touching feel good, but during her surrogate training, she had learned how to enjoy the experience of touching others. Thus she was not totally dependent upon another's skills and responses to make her feel good.

This was a breakthrough! It was now clear that Jay's silence was a cover-up for his fears about getting close. Now the unresolved issues surrounding Jay's divorce and the denial of his need for emotional closeness could be addressed constructively in therapy. Concurrently, Jay and Ann would continue in their client/surrogate relationship working to improve both Jay's sexual capacities and his capacity for intimacy.

Privately Jay confided to me that he was getting to like Ann a lot but did not know what to do about it. I encouraged Jay to tell her just how he was feeling, reminding him that there would be no chance to do that after the therapy was over. He needed to make the most of this opportunity.

I would be there in our joint therapy sessions to help Jay and Ann end their relationship when that time came. I knew, and Ann knew, that when Jay had developed more confidence in being able to relate intimately to a woman, both sexually and emotionally, that separation could take place without undue pain.

❦

When I first established the Center for Social and Sensory Learning, a Los Angeles sex therapy clinic specializing in the use of surrogate partners for single men and women, my focus was intimacy in sexual relationships, not just the reversal of sexual problems. My view was that even a one-night stand could be intimate. It all had to do with having a positive view of sexuality, self-esteem, and respect for one's partner. I was excited about the prospect of using surrogates as part of sex therapy because only through the trial and error of experience have people been able to learn about sexuality. As with any other physical skill, book learning isn't enough. But this was the first time that experiential learning in the sexual realm had the chance of becoming a socially acceptable model.

Masters and Johnson shocked the world with the publication of *Human Sexual Inadequacy*, in which they wrote of their successful use of a new experiential therapy called sensate focus. With this method, couples were able to overcome sexual problems far more successfully than with talk therapy alone.

When these successes became known, many single men expected to be able to use similar methods for their problems. To Masters and Johnson the only solution was to provide surrogate partners. In explaining his reason for so doing, Dr. Masters stated: single dysfunctional males are "societal cripples....If they are not treated, it is discrimination of one segment of society over another" (*Time*, May 25, 1970, p. 49).

At that time, providing sex therapy partners was both controversial and courageous. Dr. Masters was not, however, courageous enough to offer single women the same opportunity as men. He felt that both the professional community and the public at large would not accept that radical a breach of what seemed to be the prevailing morality. But Masters and Johnson's first step had opened the door for surrogates subsequently to be used with anyone who had a sexual problem: men, women, gay, straight, couples, the disabled, sex offenders—even teenagers!

Following Masters and Johnson's example, a handful of therapists began specializing in sex therapy using the new sensate focus approach, and here and there therapists also began to use surrogate partners to assist in the therapy. The use of surrogates was the wave of the future, and I decided to get in on the ground floor.

I had been a psychotherapist for over ten years, but being a staunch believer in experience as the best teacher, I decided that I needed to work as a surrogate myself before I could train and supervise others as surrogates. Therefore, I participated in the first surrogate training program ever conducted, a weekend of sensate focus exercises, held in San Bernardino, California. Rudimentary as it was, it was a great start. Thereafter I offered my services as a surrogate to several therapists in the Los Angeles area. While there was a good deal of theoretical information available about human sexuality, how to use this information to help clients working with surrogate partners was not yet developed. In the beginning it was necessary for surrogates and therapists to work closely together to establish the standards for this new type of therapy.

My first client was a man with multiple sclerosis. At age thirty-two he had never ever touched or been touched by a woman in an affectionate way. This was to be my ultimate test. First I had to teach Bill to wipe the drool from his chin. My second task was to protect myself, in the midst of a close embrace, from the spastic flailing of Bill's arms, hands, head, and legs. Interestingly Bill's spastic reactions were less frequent and less intense once I had begun a body caress. I was also surprised, and delighted, that he was able to learn enough about pleasing a woman that there was a good chance he would be able to relate sexually to other women of his choice.

Working as a surrogate with my second client turned out to be a great privilege. The therapist had only told me that this fifty-eight-year-old man was "inexperienced." Seeing Neil once a week for a month, I followed all of the therapist's instructions for teaching the ABCs of sex. Then Neil said he had a secret he could no longer keep.

Neil was a Catholic priest. He told me of the agony he had gone through making the decision to go to a sex therapist and asking to work with a surrogate. For many years he had counseled couples regarding their marital and sexual relationships. He felt that he was a compassionate and understanding person. He had been trained for this work. Yet, not knowing what an intimate sexual relationship was like from his own personal experience, he had always felt inadequate in his counseling.

With me he was breaking his vows of celibacy. He had very consciously chosen to do so and was glad that he had done so. However, he did not know whether he would reveal this fact in confession.

Neil's rationale was that this experience with me was a necessary part of his education, not just a personal sexual adventure. Only under the supervision of a qualified sex therapist would he allow himself to do this. I certainly was not one to judge his decision, nor had the therapist who also had been taken into Neil's confidence. Even if Neil's motive had been pure lust rather than education, I would have felt that a great honor had been bestowed upon me for being chosen to share in this momentous event.

After working as a surrogate with several other clients who had various problems, including premature ejaculation, impotence, delayed orgasm, and lack of desire, I felt ready to open my own sex therapy clinic. While Masters and Johnson had shown that using surrogates was much more successful than just talking about sex, it was still far from being an accepted professional practice. After all, wasn't it providing sex for money? And wasn't that the same as prostitution? Didn't that make me a madam? I often had to answer these accusations. I was continuously being bombarded with requests for interviews and TV appearances. And I took on all comers in order to have the opportunity to explain what surrogate-assisted sex therapy was really all about.

There are several major differences between what a surrogate does and what we typically think of a prostitute doing. Frequently a prostitute provides only the sexual experiences that are asked of her. In many cases her job is simply to provide instant gratification. She may never see the client again.

A surrogate's main purpose, rather than just to provide sexual pleasure, is to educate the client in how to reverse specific sexual problems. And it is the therapist, not the surrogate or the client, who decides what activities are appropriate in view of the overall therapy. A course of therapy is likely to take several months or more. And, in most cases, sex (defined as genital stimulation and orgasm) is the least of it.

The fact that money is paid—for the services of a prostitute, a surrogate, or a sex therapist—is not the issue. We live in a society where monetary exchange for goods and services is the rule. The intent of those who insist upon comparing surrogate-assisted sex therapy with prostitution is to demean and discredit both. It is a reflection of our basically repressive culture regarding sexuality.

As to me being a madam, I was so confident that my use of surrogate partners was therapeutically advantageous that I didn't give it a second thought. Only after twelve years of practice did we have a minor crisis at the center. After several talk sessions with me, I assigned a young man to work with a surrogate in hopes of reversing his problem of reduced sexual desire. In the middle of his first session with the surrogate, the man burst into my office telling me that he was on the vice squad and that he needed to ward off a planned raid on the center. During just the first half hour with the surrogate, he had become convinced that we were a legitimate sex therapy clinic, not a front for anything against the law. That was the end of that!

Being thought of as a madam was so far-fetched that it really was not a problem for me at all. Nevertheless, some people were convinced that being a sex therapist automatically implied having prurient interests. For me it was not uncommon at social gatherings for people to hold me at arms' length because they were intimidated by my expertise. Sometimes I would be "hit on" in hopes of getting a free lesson in sexuality. Then there were the inevitable snide sexual jokes, which showed that my companions, many of them professionals, were not always that comfortable in confronting the subject of sexuality in a candid manner.

None of these things daunted my determination to become the very best sex therapist I possibly could. Helping people accept and respect their sexual urges as a natural part of life and helping them to have satisfying sex lives was compelling for me. As a child I'd had several sexual experiences initiated by adult men. There had been no violence nor threats of violence. Yet I was sworn to secrecy and knew, from an uneasy place deep inside, that this was not socially acceptable behavior. The most traumatic part, however, was that I was blamed for being seductive and made to feel guilty.

From that time on I searched for understanding about this most powerful of human energy: sex. I observed, asked questions, read everything I could get my hands on, and experimented wherever I could. In order to learn even more I talked my husband into having an open relationship for a short while, in which either of us could, by mutual agreement, have other sexual partners. From all my searching I could only conclude there was something radically wrong with the attitude toward sex in our culture. The most important thing I discovered was that, despite the fact that we are continually being bombarded by sexual images and sexual innuendo, our society basically denies the value and beauty of sexuality. Therefore we are taught very little about it, being left to discover what little we can, through a great deal of fumbling and bumbling and embarrassment.

What masquerades as sexual freedom is often only a rebellion against the lies, secrecy, hypocrisy, and ignorance about sex that our culture imposes upon us. We have been given the message that our sexual urges and attractions are bad. They are not. They are natural and beautiful. However, in our ignorance, how we act upon those urges is often what turns the sublime into the horrific!

Sex therapy utilizing experiential methods and surrogate partners became for me a way of making sex right both for myself and for my clients. I also hoped my work might have a redeeming influence upon some of the negative sexual attitudes in our culture.

❦

In the beginning the only people interested in becoming surrogates were those who had taken the same weekend course as I had.

As could be expected, these were people who were quite comfortable with their own sexuality. They were caught up in the ideals of the sexual revolution. Most had come through the struggle of overcoming their own sexual hang-ups and problems and wanted to pass on their knowledge and skills to others. Together we began establishing techniques that we felt would be the most successful in helping clients. We worked not only with those who had specific problems, such as premature ejaculation or trouble having orgasm, but also with clients who were simply naive about sex or were having difficulty in establishing meaningful relationships.

As surrogate-assisted therapy began to prove its effectiveness and gained more acceptance, more surrogates were needed. Also, as we learned more about the clinical dynamics of the client-surrogate relationship, it was obvious that rigorous, professionally supervised training was necessary. In response, I organized the first ongoing training program for surrogates in the Los Angeles area. Likewise, there were training programs conducted by therapists in San Francisco, New York, Chicago, Toronto, San Diego, and other metropolitan areas. The International Professional Surrogates Association also established its training, as did a gay psychologist in Los Angeles, for gay surrogates.

The training program I established at the Center for Social and Sensory Learning included both men and women from their twenties into their sixties. Course requirements consisted of a minimum of seventy-two hours of both didactic and experiential learning, including class attendance, home assignments, a supervised internship, and continuing on-the-job training.

Although Masters and Johnson had not used male surrogates, the policy of the center was that women deserved the same opportunities for experiential sex therapy as men and that this was professionally viable. In the sexual realm, as in so many others, most women had not yet gained the same freedoms as most men.

Thus, fewer women took advantage of the education they could receive through surrogate therapy. Also, women were rebelling against being defined by the standards of male sexuality. In order to help women define themselves sexually, at times we had a female surrogate work with a female client, even when both were heterosexually oriented. As a result of our policy, we always had several women clients in therapy, some with a female surrogate, some with a male surrogate.

Wendy was one of these women. Wendy thought that she was incapable of having orgasms. She told me that her ex-boyfriend had tried everything. So many times she would be right on the edge, but nothing ever happened. Her boyfriend accused her of holding out on him. In a way she was because she wouldn't let go. She was holding on for dear life, afraid to surrender.

Wendy had always felt that men were doing something *to* her to *make* her respond. That made her tense and angry. She hated the idea of *giving in*. That felt like defeat instead of joy. In her experience men had always called the shots during sex, and she thought that was what made it easy for them to have orgasms. Wendy claimed to like sex and wanted to have orgasms, but for her it had become a power struggle. She blamed both her partner and herself. She was desperately confused.

Chuck was Wendy's surrogate. I had them spend a lot of time just caressing for the pleasure of caressing. Nothing more. Each session they caressed a different part of the body: hands, face, feet, back, and front (excluding genitals at first). Since Chuck wasn't putting pressure on her to respond in any particular way, Wendy began to learn that there could be a lot more to sex than orgasm. I reminded her that she had told me "nothing ever happened" during sex. She had been so focused upon trying to have an orgasm that she had missed out on all the fun of hugging, kissing, and caressing.

I asked Wendy if she liked dancing because moving to rhythmic music is a lot like surrendering to one's feelings during lovemaking. As might be expected, she felt inhibited dancing. After much probing, I discovered that Wendy was learning to ski. During her previous lesson, she had mustered up the courage to go over a small hill where she could not see what was on the other side. It was frightening, but once over the crest the skis automatically carried her safely down to level ground. She was exhilarated.

I told Wendy that a similar exhilaration could come from letting go into her orgasm. It was not a question of "giving in" to her partner but surrendering to the sensations within her body—surrendering to the process of lovemaking. I assured Wendy that making love does not have to be something people do *to* each other but rather it should and can be an ecstatic blending in the fulfillment of mutual desires. But first she would have to learn what her desires are and then how to ask her partner for what she wants. This was difficult for Wendy, but finally when she was able to communicate openly with Chuck about what pleased her, she was able to let go into her own feeling of pleasure and then into her own orgasm. By the end of therapy she felt confident enough to initiate sex again with her old boyfriend and help release him from the pressure of thinking he was not a good lover because he couldn't make her have an orgasm. Thus their power struggle was resolved, and the boyfriend learned a thing or two from Wendy as well.

❦

From personal experimentation and my sex therapy practice, I learned a lot, not only about the physical aspects of sex but also about the importance of values, attitudes, expectations, and hidden assumptions.

Paul came to therapy to overcome impotence. He was seventy-two years old but had never before had a problem. He was filled with shame and despair. His wife, Janet, had recently been diagnosed with Parkinson's disease. Paul admitted that he was afraid that lovemaking might not be as acceptable to her as in the past. That, in itself, was a probable contributing factor for his impotence.

During our first session, Janet asked him, "But why did you move into the guest room?" Paul, stuttering and obviously wondering how she could possibly ask such a question, replied, "Why can't you understand? I've told you: I just can't get it up anymore." Janet replied, in just as annoyed a tone of voice, "Yes, I know, but that shouldn't stop us from cuddling!"

Obviously they had a major conflict of values. Paul did not know any way to express his love and affection other than through intercourse. Janet felt deprived because Paul refused any physical closeness. Paul felt cuddling would be too arousing, and since he had no way of following through, that it would be frustrating for both.

Both Paul and Janet had a lot to learn about the physical aspects of sex, even after almost fifty years of marriage, but their assumptions and expectations had to be confronted first. Because the tension was so great between them, with Janet's permission, I had Paul work with a surrogate. In this way he could learn the value of cuddling, with or without an erection. And, since the pressure was off, he could also learn how to let his erections come naturally again. Then I had Paul and Janet do some of the exercises at home together. Gradually he learned that there are more ways to express love then always having a hard and long-lasting erection. Janet learned that what she wanted as expressions of loving attention did not always meet the expectations and needs of her husband. Therefore, she also had to learn new ways of satisfying her husband, which, at the same time, did not endanger her fragile health. Paul and Janet were back in bed together. And for both, the myth had been exploded that the only way to show love and affection or to allay sexual and emotional frustration is through intercourse and orgasm.

Learning about the expectations, hopes, and fears that underlie the concerns the client expresses at the beginning of therapy is made much easier with the assistance of a surrogate partner. Because the client and the surrogate have had no prior relationship, there are no vested interests to protect, and no ingrained habits of how they relate to one another to overcome. That allows each of them to be more open, more candid, and more vulnerable with each other. Thus, what has been hidden, even to the client, or kept secret for some reason can be brought out into the open. That enables all three of us, the client, the surrogate, and the therapist, to learn many things that are of great importance to the success of the therapy.

One client, a policeman in his late twenties, was still a virgin. Vern had many inhibitions, but with the help of Marion, his surrogate, he slowly overcame them. In fact, Vern did not even have the basic social skills. So, I had him take Marion out on several pretend dates. Only after that did they get to the bodywork. After several more weeks, when all of the preliminary touching exercises had been done, I gave the assignment for Vern and Marion to take turns giving each other a front-body caress, including casually touching the genitals. I emphasized that they were not to concentrate upon the genitals for the purpose of arousal or orgasm but merely to include them as just another part of the body.

When it was time for feedback with me, Vern was distraught. As he walked into my office, he was apologizing profusely to Marion. He felt guilty because in touching her genitals, she had not had an orgasm. His deeply ingrained beliefs about how sex is supposed to be were now surfacing. And my very specific instructions about not striving for orgasm had bounced right off him. What emerged was the belief that touching genitals should automatically lead to instant orgasm, and that he was totally responsible for producing that response in his partner. Now, having this hidden belief exposed, Vern had gotten to one of the main causes for his fear of initiating sexual relationships. The imagined responsibility was too much for him.

But what was of more importance, in the long run, was discovering through the initial emphasis on Vern's sexual problems that Vern was intimidated by women in every way. He had gotten the message in his childhood that men were expected to wait upon women hand and foot and always give in to their desires. This was the imagined responsibility that was too much for Vern. After this burden had been relieved in therapy, not only did Vern's sex life radically improve, but also his life with parents, friends, and on the job. In fact, this was the case for most clients. Since sex is usually the one aspect of a person's life that is kept the most secret and is the most fraught with conflict, if one confronts and solves sexual problems, then coping with the other aspects of life becomes easier.

No matter what problem the client presents as being of immediate importance, a basic lesson to be learned is that we all must be responsible for our own pleasure and our own orgasms. We cannot expect our partner to do it all for us, and then if things don't go the way we like, blame the other person.

To learn how to take responsibility for ourselves and then to share our pleasure with a partner can be learned. The secret is to pay attention to how we feel when we are touching our partner rather than thinking about whether we are doing it right. If we are touching in a way that pleases ourselves, most always that will be pleasing to our partner. If not, our partner has the responsibility of letting us know. This way there is no guessing or pretending or blaming, and trust is built. And no, it is not selfish, because when we fill our own well of pleasure to overflowing, the pleasure will then flow from us to our partner. But learning these things takes practice, and everyone does not always have a willing and knowledgeable companion with whom to practice. That is why the role of the surrogate is so important. Again, these are lessons for improving life in general, not just for improving one's sex life.

In working with hundreds of people over a period of more than two decades, it has become evident that the individual problems of clients are merely reflective of the problems surrounding sexuality in the culture in which we live.

Every social culture from the beginning of time has regulated sexual activity for the purpose of maintaining stability in the society. It has been shown from the studies of primitive cultures that a society that had both unambiguous and open attitudes toward sexuality had less violence within that society and less violence toward other peoples than in more repressive cultures.

In modern Western societies the messages about sex are extremely contradictory and confusing. We have no traditional rites of passage nor meaningful ceremonies to initiate young people into informed adult sexuality. I hoped that my work might establish standards that could help people of all ages have less confusion about sex and intimate relationships. Much to my professional satisfaction, there were several enlightened parents who paid for a full course of surrogate-assisted therapy so that their sons could be initiated into the wonders of their own sexuality. How lucky to have subsequently been those young men's girlfriends or wives! I often wished that parents would take that same enlightened view toward sexual initiation for their daughters, but it was not yet the time for that. I predict, however, that that day will eventually come.

Until recently, the message was very strong that sex should be limited to marriage and monogamy. Yet everyone knows this standard is continuously being broken. But more often than not, it is broken in secrecy and with guilt. Our standards are very hypocritical. What we say and what we do just don't jibe.

We are led to believe through the incessant references to sex in the media that we live in a society that condones open sexuality, but when examined more closely, most of what is shown on TV, in the movies, or in print is labeled "X-rated" or "for adults only," which implies that the sexual activities depicted are really not OK. And, although sexual innuendo sells everything from baby lotion to trucks, the link between sex and violence is more prevalent than the seductive soft sell.

The number of children sexually abused, the number of teenage pregnancies, the spread of AIDS, the high incidence of rape, and the millions of people who are unhappy in their sex lives shows that in our supposedly open and free culture things have really gotten out of hand. The authorities who shape our attitudes toward sex attempt to make us believe that these problems are caused by too much openness toward sexuality. Just the opposite is true. It is the unwarranted sexual repression that causes sexual exploitation and aberrant behavior. Both the stifling of sexuality and the inevitable rebellion against prudery and ignorance is what puts us at the mercy of our sexual urges rather than being personally in charge of our sexuality.

I have said that sex is natural and beautiful. But there is a flip side to believing that sex is natural. Bob was very reluctant to come for help. He had two older brothers who were always boasting about their sexual exploits. Bob, however, couldn't seem to get to first base with women. He felt very awkward, not ever knowing what to say or do. He thought that something must be terribly wrong with him because he expected that when he was with a woman, everything would just happen naturally. Bob firmly believed that because sex is a natural biological function that there is no need to talk about it nor learn about it. And if he hadn't finally learned more about sex by some means or another, all of Bob's pent-up sexual urges and feelings of frustration might have violently exploded without his intent. The help of a surrogate saved him from such a plight. Bob was astounded by all the wonderful things there were to know about sex and realized that ignorance is not bliss.

Using the argument that sex is natural and therefore need not be discussed and taught in the schools, on TV, or in surrogate-assisted therapy is most often just a cover for the attitude that any reference to sex is sinful. What in reality *is* sinful is *not* talking about sex, *not* respecting and honoring our natural sexual feelings. Condemning and preventing all attempts to learn what sex is really all about is actually the root of the evil.

What is desperately needed are clear, unambiguous standards of sexual behavior that support the responsible and joyous expression of our sexuality. But this cannot be achieved in theory only. Such standards can only become effective through societally approved experiential learning. Surrogate-assisted therapy has proven to serve that purpose.

❦

An example of how confused cultural standards take their toll can be seen in Saul's story. Saul's wife had recently walked out on him. She called him a sex maniac. He was angry. He thought it was his right to have sex with his wife whenever he wanted. He didn't understand why his wife didn't accept that when he was horny, he *needed* to relieve himself; it was not a matter of choice. It seemed that he was horny all the time. In fact, the more his wife rejected him, the hornier he got. And masturbation was for Saul an unacceptable substitute, even once in a while. He had been taught that masturbation was bad. He did it, sometimes, but only because he *had* to.

In therapy, at first, all Saul could do was vent his anger, and he kept trying to get me to tell him that he was justified. I told Saul that I didn't think many women would go along with his sexual demands but that he could learn to be the boss over his strong sex drive rather than letting it rule him. Saul was shocked when he realized that, in truth, he wasn't in charge of himself, but he was afraid that if he went along with my suggestions, he would lose his sex drive. However, he seemed to have no other choice than to give sex therapy a chance.

Saul was amazed to learn that he could turn his sexual energy on and off at will. He could increase it or decrease it. He could move it around into different parts of his body. And with his surrogate he discovered that he could have a satisfaction that was far more than just physical release. In one of the exercises I assigned, I had Saul's surrogate repeatedly stimulate him to just the edge of orgasm and then disperse the sexual energy into other places in his body. Then just before the end of the session, she stimulated him to orgasm. Saul discovered that he did not need to suffer the intense frustration he had felt in the past when he didn't get the instant release that he thought he had to have. In this process, Saul's rigid ideas about sex were replaced by his own personal experience, which gave him much more control over his sexuality and at the same time a feeling of more sexual freedom. He was no longer locked into his self-imposed limitations. No amount of trying to talk Saul into believing that there was another way could have done that.

But how surrogates can possibly work with angry clients like Saul is an often asked question. How can surrogates be caring and understanding with clients they not only don't know but may not even like? Everyone has at least one likable trait and surrogates find those traits in their clients. They have been trained to look beyond the surface into the vulnerable essence which is in all of us. But many clients do have characteristics that could put anyone off, just as many of the rest of us do. For instance, a client may be an incorrigible pessimist, always complaining about everything. The surrogate, understandably, could be both angered and discouraged by this behavior. These are real-life feelings. But with the therapist as monitor, in the same way as with married couples, there is a chance of resolving whatever feelings may come up between the client and the surrogate. In this way the client can learn more effective methods of communication, which can be used in subsequent relationships. It is, in fact, the irritating traits of clients and the difficulties in the client-surrogate relationship that serve as grist for the therapeutic process.

Another safeguard for the surrogate, and the client too, is that because they have not known each other previously, they are not emotionally entangled with each other. That allows the surrogate and the client to have more objectivity. In addition, the temporary nature of the therapy allows for authentic emotional involvement without the danger of becoming too dependent upon each other. Also, of utmost importance, surrogates must have their needs for intimacy and sex met in their personal relationships outside of the client-surrogate relationship. And most clients are not looking for a permanent relationship with a surrogate, but rather are looking forward to establishing relationships of their own choice, also outside of the client-surrogate relationship. These factors enable surrogates to wholeheartedly play the role of helper and for clients to accept that help without feeling any pressure to meet the needs of the surrogate.

Finally, the close monitoring of the developing relationship between surrogate and client, by the therapist, provides protection for both the client and the surrogate from inappropriate and potentially damaging emotions. Further protection is provided by the therapist's role as negotiator in dealing with the feelings involved in the separation process at the completion of therapy.

For those who were not familiar with these built-in protections for both the client and the surrogate, the most loaded question ever asked was: "What if the client and the surrogate fall in love?" as if falling in love were the worst possible fate. This question was intended to imply that it was likely that the client, being in a vulnerable position, would become overly dependent upon the surrogate and therefore be emotionally damaged. Thus this question alone was meant to invalidate the whole premise of surrogate-assisted therapy. My answer always was: "I hope they do fall in love." That was a bit facetious, but in all seriousness I did expect that the client and the surrogate would develop closeness, caring, love, and respect for each other! For the client, the relationship with the surrogate may be the first opportunity, ever, to experience what intimacy is all about! And hopefully for both, despite the inevitable difficult aspects, the relationship will have been both enjoyable and rewarding.

Unfortunately, the use of surrogates as assistants in sex therapy has declined during the past few years, mainly due to the influence of sexual repression in our society and the fear of venereal disease and AIDS. The decline in the use of surrogates, for these reasons, need not be. The guidelines of safe-sex can be used and the physical contact between the client and surrogate can stop short of penetration and the exchange of body fluids. Ninety-nine percent of what clients need to know about sexuality and intimacy can be learned far short of having intercourse. When the public learns about the unequaled value of surrogate-assisted therapy, demands for the use of surrogates will undoubtedly influence therapists to incorporate them into their practice more frequently.

While surrogate partners have been used primarily as adjuncts in therapy for those with sexual problems, it gradually became clear to me that what was being taught is of universal value. The training for surrogates and clients alike imparts knowledge about healthy sexual relationships that can apply to everyone. It was this realization which led me to offer the Sexual Enrichment Experience, a class for people who did not necessarily have specific sexual problems but who wanted to learn as much as possible to enrich their sexual relationships.

From what was discovered from the training of surrogates, working with clients with sexual problems, and the sexual enrichment program came the joining of sexuality with spirituality. This led to advanced classes, in which the sacredness of sex was the focus, using some of the ancient principles of Tantra and the Tao. Also, a few of the most experienced surrogates taught these principles to interested clients on a one-to-one basis.

Surrogate-assisted sex therapy and sexual enrichment programs are perfect models for urgently needed sex education. We now have the knowledge to create ways in which people of both genders and people of every sexual orientation can be initiated into joyous, responsible, and enlightened sexuality. All that is necessary is the demand that this knowledge be made available on a widespread basis. May that day come in the very near future!

❦

Four months before the publication of Women of the Light, *Barbara Roberts died. She had written her chapter during a period when her cancer was in remission. A month before her last breath, she wrote a letter to many of her friends, part of which is reprinted here:*

Since my diagnosis of lung cancer six years ago, I have been successfully fighting to stay alive and to have as much quality of life as possible.

Clinging to hope for a physical cure at this time is false hope. But I do hope that my death can be pain free and peaceful. However, full acceptance means letting go of even that.

Coming to the truth about my life and my death has already made me feel more at peace. I no longer have that awful feeling of not knowing what the future holds. The future holds the death of my physical body and yes I do believe the continuation of my spirit. Knowing this, I am now free to ponder about how I wish my death to be. Much of that is out of my hands. What I can do is touch base with you and say good-bye.

In the afternoon of June 2, 1994, Barbara awoke, looked at her son and her daughter holding her hands, took a deep breath and let it out, and then took one more short breath as she died peacefully.

JWALA

❦

THE MEDITATION
TEACHER

Introduction to

JWALA

Jwala arrived exhausted at my door. She had just driven up from Los Angeles to teach a seminar here in the San Francisco Bay Area. In her usual gypsylike lifestyle, she was carrying in her blue ten-year-old Chevy sedan most of her worldly possessions, including a prized musical instrument, a large tambura from India, the country where she has spent many of her recent winters following the sun and her spiritual quest.

Jwala (pronounced jeh-WAH-lah) is a meditation teacher, though not of the kind most would think. She is a sexual-meditation teacher. Generally meditation is characterized by attentiveness and mindfulness. More relaxation and inner peace often accompany. In her seminars and individual sessions, Jwala teaches how to bring these qualities into the sexual expression. Ceremony and sensuality are central. Friction sex and "slam, bam, thank you, ma'am" are replaced by *sacred sex*, the title she selected for her recent book.

Jwala is a Tantrika, a follower of Tantra, which is the name for several similar spiritual traditions coming from some schools of Hinduism and Buddhism. *Tantra* is a Sanskrit term sometimes considered to be derived from translations of *to weave*, sometimes from a combination of *to expand* and *to liberate*. The Tantric philosophy expresses views often in sharp contrast to those of ascetics and hedonists.

Asceticism, a strong undercurrent in many fundamentalist religious belief systems, considers anything that is pleasing to the senses as obstructive of or destructive to spiritual attainment. Pleasures of the flesh are addictive or make no real contribution to the individual and society. One must abstain and avoid; sometimes self-inflicted pain is believed to make the follower more deserving of God's mercy. To the ascetic, there is something inherently negative or evil about the body; combining *sacred* and *sex* into a single concept would be blasphemy. After yielding to temptation, one must seek atonement.

In hedonism, quite to the contrary, one intensely pursues gratification of desires. There is a grasping attempt to consume. Without continued titillation of the senses, life looses its luster. An ascetic pointing a finger at such behavior would label a hedonist as indulgent, decadent, and narcissistic.

In contrast to asceticism and hedonism, Tantra teaches neither to damn nor to crave the body and the senses. Rather than being obstacles, our sensations and feelings become the vehicles of spiritual growth when we embrace the sensory experiences and transform their energies through meditative practices.

This philosophy encourages full participation in all aspects of life, including our sexuality. In Tantric sacred sex we honor the Divine within ourself, our partner, and the cosmos. Conscious choice and consent are primary. We shift from *sin, guilt, evil*, and *addiction* to *love, joy, compassion*, and *equanimity*. We seek *at-one-ment*, not *atonement*. In Tantra we celebrate the heart and the senses.

This is what Jwala teaches. And when she arrived at my door to be my houseguest during her series of seminars in the Bay Area, I was indeed looking forward to hearing of her travels, insights, and gurus in India. I had had profound experiences studying with a Tibetan lama in residence in America but had never visited the lands and peoples from which Tantra had originated. The next hour I was to learn nonverbally more about Jwala and Tantra than from all our talks during the friendship that was to follow.

Seeing Jwala's exhaustion, I invited her to lie down on her back there on the living room carpet for a few minutes of massage beginning with the muscles on her neck and upper back. Perhaps for half an hour the massage continued, my hands being continually drawn toward her heart area. To complete, I lay one of my hands on top of her heart area while the other cradled her neck. Slowly I lifted my hands from her physical body and remained sitting cross-legged in meditation near the top of her head. Sensing her energetic field with mine, I relaxed into our connection.

A moaninglike sound began to emerge from Jwala as an explosion of energy shook my body. I heard her volume intensify and opened my eyes just enough to see her upper body arching. We were both entering a state of energetic orgasm—fully clothed, with no seductive intents, no erogenous zone touching.

Except for a few phone calls and one five-minute face-to-face introduction, Jwala and I were strangers. For years both of us had been meditators with sexuality at the center of our spiritual paths. And now our energetic bodies were making love in ways that masters of Tantra, Taoism, and other mystical traditions have described over the ages.

To understand the sacred prostitute, we have to be open to the possibility that *sex* is more than and sometimes other than penis-vagina intercourse, oral-genital congress, anal intercourse, or masturbation. Sex can be an energetic dance. In the ancient temples where sex was a sacrament, learning how to develop and direct the "subtle, energetic bodies" was likely often a part of the esoteric knowledge passed on to initiates of the priest/esshood. What to us may look like "getting laid" was often actually a form of laying-on-of-hands healing. One went to the sacred prostitute to become transformed—to be born again.

Though Jwala thinks of herself as a teacher of the sensual/sexual arts rather than a sacred prostitute, she knows and seeks this mystical, energetic dance. Yet following this path, "the path of fire" as she calls it, means paying a price. Because she has chosen to be openly sexually free, she has encountered oppressive responses from authoritarian men and women and institutions. She knows, however, that the price of submitting to repressive regimes of the mind and body is far greater. So she continues to seek. Her spirit must dance. Others who wish to be free, she invites to join her dance. Many of us have. And for this, we are enriched.

THE MEDITATION TEACHER

by

Jwala

I was born in Boston to a dentist and a housewife. Soon my father joined the military and we were stationed here, there, and everywhere. Change became a part of my life, and I had to learn to make new friends wherever we landed. My parents didn't go to church, but I was told that I was a Protestant. I went to church because I liked singing the hymns. After the service one Sunday, I joined the congregation mingling outside. What I overheard seemed so trivial. The women were talking about one another's outfits, and the men were talking about cars and the prices of things. I was so turned off and disillusioned that I stopped going to church. One hour of piety followed by a week of mundane trivialities seemed to me the height of hypocrisy.

Around this same time I remember my first conscious awareness of my sexual energy. It was at my twelfth birthday party, and we were playing a kissing game. The boys all sat in chairs, and the girls came and sat on their laps to give them a kiss. The boy would say, "Pass," and you'd move on to the next boy. If he said, "Fail," you'd stay and give him another kiss. Friends couldn't believe I wasn't worried about my parents coming down and what they might think. I jokingly said, "Are you kidding? They fight and get drunk and argue. How could they object to us being down here having such a good time?"

Years seemed to pass by with only a few crushes and make-out sessions. I was an enthusiastic teenager for the most part, and I channeled a lot of my sexual energy into sports, artwork, and being a cheerleader.

At sixteen, I had my first religious experience while staying at my girlfriend's house. I was upstairs in the guest room, and all of a sudden I was hit with a bolt of white light and fell onto the bed. A loving presence filled my body and Jesus was there. I felt an incredible calling to serve people, yet I didn't have a clue how that would later manifest.

My next spiritual inspiration happened at eighteen when Up With People, a spiritual singing group, came to town to perform. This is a group that aspires to four principles: honesty, purity, unselfishness, and love. Its message is the unification of humanity. I knew I had to be with them, but my parents said no because I had had a chronic skin disease for two years. I was so determined to go,

I sought out a healing and found a new doctor. Within weeks, I was healed.

Shortly, I joined the traveling show and loved the singing and dancing and meeting new people. There was no dating in the group, but after a year with them I began to fancy one of the men in the company. We talked, joked, and sometimes took walks together. Then one day I was called in and reprimanded for my association with him. I was outraged. We were being natural and innocent. We never did anything overtly sexual and had great energy for each other (years later he was the first man to propose to me). Very upset, I left the group after that scolding because I felt something was unnatural there. Little did I know the trouble this free, wild-spirited woman would encounter for expressing such naturally erotic, open, loving, innocent energy.

Another favorite man, whom I'd dated since age seventeen, kept in touch with me by letters and phone calls. We started getting closer and seeing each other more often. Finally he decided to get a job in my town for the summer so we could be close to each other. I loved this man and had known him for four years. We'd been told by his parents that we had to wait until marriage before having intercourse. I didn't see why we should wait anymore and wanted to go all the way, so I went down to the health clinic and bought some birth control pills. Finally at age twenty-one, we two virgins did it! It felt wonderful, and I couldn't believe that we had waited so long. Needless to say, neither of us knew anything about sex, being virgins groping in the dark. Then I began to wonder why we hadn't been taught about sex, since it seemed to be an important thing in our lives and almost everyone else's. After a while I realized that I seldom had an orgasm since it took me so much more time to get ignited than my partner.

Within a few months, my boyfriend met the woman of his dreams in the park and wrote me a "Dear John" letter. I was shocked and hurt. I knew this was no way to end such a long and deep love relationship. I wanted a more compassionate way to disconnect, so I called him and we spent our last weekend together. He was definitely no longer available to me.

Luckily, my spiritual growth was in full swing. At twenty, I had been introduced to 3HO kundalini yoga: hatha yoga positions with fast nostril breathing. I don't recall feeling so "high" from anything before. Also, I began studying the graceful movements of Tai Chi and Chi Kung. The next year I began taking metaphysical classes at the Teaching of the Inner Christ and became more body-mind-spirit aware. This spiritual group not only gave me a spiritual foundation, but it also embraced positive sexuality.

Then I had an experience that would change my life forever. I met a man on the beach, and he asked me if I'd like a massage the following week. He arrived in the afternoon on Wednesday and told me to take off all my clothes. I was suspicious for a few moments but then relaxed because I really wanted to be touched. He had learned, sensual hands, and my body drank in his touch like a sponge. He touched me in places I was barely aware of—in between my toes, on my "third eye," on my perineum, which he gently pressed. He spent hours giving pleasure to me without sexually coming on to me. When he finished, he kissed me on my forehead and quietly left. Who was he and how did he know how to touch me so exquisitely? I found a fountain in his fingertips. We began to date. He was a fantastic lover, giving me lots of foreplay, so slow and deliberate, and I started having orgasms more often. Finally I said, "You don't seem to be in a hurry to get done with lovemaking like a lot of men. You are so gentle and giving." He said he'd been studying Tantra with a local couple. They turned out to be graduates of the Teaching of the Inner Christ, where I had been studying recently.

Within weeks, he took me to my first Tantra teachers. Sensitive, tasteful people, they took me under their wing. They stripped me to the bare essentials—nudity on all levels. They began by massaging away my body armoring, a term introduced by Wilhelm Reich. First, both of them together would massage me for several hours with long, deep strokes. Then she would leave and he'd say, "Now I'm going to erotically turn you on, and I don't want you to move a muscle or strive to come. I'm going to bring you to orgasm even if it takes two days." Well, all kinds of emotions came up to block my pleasure, mostly feelings of rage toward my father, which came out in crying and screaming. Similar sessions continued each week with much resistance on my part. I was able to follow his instructions to breathe into my genitals and just let go into orgasm. Finally I did, and I exploded into pure consciousness, white-light egolessness, no-mind…bliss.

Such ecstasy I'd never known before, although it was somewhat similar to the spiritual visitation by Jesus when I was sixteen. With this orgasmic ecstasy began my integration of the concept that sex and spirit are one energy, our very life force. Tantra is a teaching that harnesses pleasure, vision, and ecstasy—celebrating them rather than repressing them. *Tantra* stands for the view that sexual energy is a divine, all-encompassing life force that sleeps within the individual, permeates the universe, and affects everything we do from birth to death. As sexual beings, we have the ability to raise that energy within ourselves and use it to directly experience altered or mystical states of consciousness. In effect, we become "gods" and "goddesses," our bodies transformed into temples of male and female divinity.

Another turning point in my life came after an evening when I attended a Tantra class and then went to a political meeting. At the end of the intensely blissful Tantra class, the teacher had said, "Now, don't disperse this incredible energy you feel among yourselves, but take it out into the world to those you meet next." I was so high and clear when I arrived at my political meeting. The evening was to train us how to handle possible confrontational situations at the next day's rally against the local nuclear plant. Within an hour my high was gone, and by the end of the meeting I had a migraine headache. That was the night I changed from the outer revolution to the inner revolution, from fear to love, from banging my head against the wall to healing my own life. Tantra became my path of surrender—my release from rigidity and struggle.

My teachers soon saw that I was very in tune with the Tantric teachings and began training me as an apprentice. I remember one of my homework assignments was to go to a party of friends and practice giving facial and head massages that I had just been taught. Part of the instruction was to focus on breathing, without getting involved in conversation. On one level, it was an experience of my unconditional love, but it had a Catch-22 along with it. In those days, almost all the receivers were men, and most of the women were too uptight or resistant to let me touch them. A week later, I heard a rumor that I was trying to steal the boyfriends of others at the party. When I heard that, I was so crushed and hurt. I cried buckets of tears. I was naive about others' potential fears and hadn't shared with people that I was doing healings and not coming on to the men. I had left the party alone, feeling so content with having shared a new skill that made people feel nurtured and pleasured.

Soon I realized that touch in our society was almost always associated with sexual come-on or meant that one had a sexual motive in mind. As I progressed, I saw that the primal need to be held and cuddled and experience physical closeness and affection is denied for the most part to many people. Therefore, the art of touch became one of my major contributions to myself, to my lovers, and to my clients.

My health co-op was meeting to take over management of a local spa. In the middle of the meeting, the manager came in hysterically shouting, "Can anyone here give a client a massage right now?" My hand raised by itself. I was ushered into a walled-off cubicle and shown where the lotion and towels were. In walked a rather uptight businessman, and I told him where he could put his clothes and that he could lie on his stomach and I would be right back. When I returned, he was face up and asked if he could get sex. I said I didn't do that, but I was new at the place and I would inquire whether anyone else there did full service. I went out to the receptionist and she said, "Do you see a sign here that says 'sex for sale'? And tell the guy he doesn't get his money back either."

Apprehensively I walked back into the cubicle and gave him the news, and continued, "So since you're here and on the table, why don't you just relax? I give a great massage, so why not try it?" He agreed with a sigh. Halfway into the massage, he started letting go and talking about the stress and upsets in his life. Within moments, I had become a psychologist with moving hands. Boy, did he unload a wad of mental and emotional stuff! No wonder he thought that sex would help him not feel his burdens. Upon completion, he looked like a new person. As he came out, he handed me a crumpled up bill and thanked me for a great session.

Years later a client came to learn Tantra, and after two sessions, he asked me if I knew of a massage therapist who would include his genitals in the massage. He said that he had gotten a no from all those he had phoned. He continued by sharing that his wife was in a foreign country because of a death in her family and he was feeling quite lonely and needed some TLC.

My first response was, "I'm sure I could find someone." The next day it dawned on me that I could do it. I felt very compassionate for his predicament, which overrode my slight feeling of nervousness. Three days later, at age thirty-eight, I did my first "sensual massage" for money. He felt very nurtured, and I felt of service.

Later the same year, while visiting Hawaii, I met my first Osho *sannyasin* (an Indian term meaning a person committed to the spiritual path). He handed me a special Tantra edition of the sannyasin magazine from India. I commented, "Oh, an Indian master not against sex, how unusual!" The sannyasin taught me an active dynamic meditation where one does heavy breathing with undulating movement, then cathartic sounds, then jumping while chanting "Hoo," next lying still or standing, and lastly celebrating with dance. After the meditation, I opened my eyes and saw light specks everywhere. Later, I learned that this is *orgone energy*, as conceptualized by Wilhelm Reich.

A few years later, in 1977, I was reexposed to Osho, a Tantric master, and began to feel a pull to go and meet him in India. Several months later, I finished my job teaching hatha yoga at a college and told them to find another instructor as I was off to India. After three weeks at the ashram, I asked to become a sannyasin. As I sat in front of Osho, he suggested that I abandon myself to my own energy. I closed my eyes and an inner ecstasy began building, my breath became deep, and loud orgasmic sounds peaked into a climax as I fell to the ground. He said, "Come back now," and gave me a new name: "Ma Prem Jwala. *Prem* means love, and *Jwala* means volcanic fire: Love Fire."

Then he continued, "The ochre color of your dress is the color of fire. To become a sannyasin is to enter into the flames of love. It is dangerous, and yet it is incredibly beautiful. Only danger is beautiful because only danger brings you to moments of joy and ecstasy. Only in danger does your life take on a kind of intensity. Then everything is intense: joy is intense, sadness is intense. All is fire. If you can pass through the fire of love, it consumes you—it consumes all that can be consumed. In the end, only a pure consciousness is left behind. So let it become your very path!"

Two days later, Osho asked me to teach Tantra yoga groups in the ashram. I had led four groups in California, so I had a little experience. But Osho told me to leave my lesson plan or structure and be more spontaneous. My first group in the ashram was only ten days later. The participants left their shoes and clothes in lockers before they entered the group room. We breathed together, sang, danced, laughed, and cried. Each of us went up in front of the group and talked about what we liked and didn't like about our naked bodies. We paired up in dyads and learned how to open and raise our sexual energy. By the end of the three-day group, most people were sparkling. I gave out red hearts at the end of the group and joked about their "heart-ons." Fifteen years later I ran into one of the women in the group from Amsterdam and she said, "I have something to show you." She lifted up her passport bag and there was the red heart I had given her, stitched onto the front. Tears came to my eyes as we hugged.

Staying in Osho's ashram in Poona, India, was a unique and profound experience for me. I fondly recall a time in 1978 when I lived in a bamboo hut and the sounds of lovemaking filled the evening air from all directions. My spiritual master would suggest that if one is *totally* making love, the whole neighborhood should hear. Outside of this special setting, I've learned some very trying lessons. My expressive sounds of love and ecstasy have not always been welcome. Being asked to leave some places because of my moans of joy, I've felt very hurt and misjudged that sounds of passionate celebration have appeared threatening to others. I've had to deal with lovers pushing pillows over my mouth, neighbors calling the police, jealous landlords, and upset roommates—all because of ecstatic sounds! "How dare you express such playful pleasure…exude so much sensuality!" For many in many cultures, ecstasy is taboo, puritanical is the path. For such a world, there is much value to be gained from Tantric teachings.

What I do as a Tantrika is to initiate people into the arts of Tantra through workshops, classes, celebrations, ceremonies, and individual or couple's sessions. As a teacher of ancient sexual secrets, I am a

catalyst to inspire the unaware to go for more aliveness and juiciness. By continuing to strive to become a more spiritually and sexually enlightened woman, I may serve as a role model for others.

When teaching, I often ask people to make a list of their top-ten
turn-ons in life, the things that inspire their total absorption and
juiciness. I then ask them to put this list up on their bathroom mirror for a week, read it every morning and evening, and notice how
much time they spend doing the things they love to do. The amount
of time is amazingly low for most people, so I invite them to start for
one hour a day doing something or a combination of items on the
list as a way to increase self-love and healing. Many students have
shared that when they started spending more time doing the things
on their list, they felt happier, less needy, and projected less on their
partner to provide so much. When people are turned on, their joy is
infectious. It is as if their cup is filling up more from the inside and
in some cases spilling over. The spilling over becomes a "give love"
rather than a "need love." For others, it begins healing the concept
that it is selfish to put the interests of oneself before the needs of
others. Osho expressed it something like this: To know oneself
requires a certain inquiry that might look selfish from a traditional
point of view.

A slightly different exercise I suggest is to make a list of the top-
ten *sexual* turn-ons, and to indicate whether they do them and communicate these erotic zones and techniques to their partner or lover.
The impact for many is great because often they don't feel they have
the right to ask for what they like sexually. The result of sharing
these likes for several clients has resulted in sexual pleasure and
fulfillment. I remember hearing my spiritual master saying that 90
percent of womankind are angry, nagging, and bitchy because their
deepest orgasmic needs are never met.

Another practice I suggest, especially to those who have a difficult time making a list of their sexual turn-ons, is to discover their

sexual turn-ons through *doing* ritualistic self-loving. My teachers suggested that we do it for an hour without coming. This was how I really discovered my erotic zones and how I liked them stimulated. I found my wrists very sensitive, my inner thighs, and the back of my neck. I learned how to create pathways for the orgasmic energy to travel throughout my whole body. From then on, especially when I was in between lovers or traveling, I enjoyed the beauty of self-pleasuring many parts of my body.

The impact of Tantric teachings on impotent men and preorgasmic women has been incredible. What I found was that healing the heart from a painful past relationship, doing certain intense breathing exercises, practicing PC and anal muscle contractions,[1] and a little loving encouragement did wonders. One married client began to get erections again after four or five sessions. By releasing old sadness and reawakening energy circuitry, many clients experience confidence and openness returning.

Working with preorgasmic women, I observed we have to go back and heal, mostly through breathwork, the trauma stored in the pelvis from early sexual roughness, abuse, or shock. The impact is dramatic as they reclaim their right to feel pleasure, to open again to trust, and to experience orgasm.

To share with couples the skills of touching and massage, how to stimulate the G spot, how to connect energetically when they might be too tired for sex, and how to set up a more erotic bedroom are all parts of my work as a Tantrika.

I feel and see that the breathwork in Tantra opens one up to the fact that we all have access to our own orgasmic energy. Because most of us thought our sexual feelings were wrong, we became

---

[1] [Ed.] Commonly referred to as the *PC muscle*, the pubococcygeus muscle surrounds the vaginal and anal orifices, contracts involuntarily during orgasm, and can be voluntarily exercised to enhance sexual functioning and pleasure.

shallow breathers. By doing this, we unconsciously learned to tone down or even turn off feeling in the sex center.

Through conscious breathing, clients can greatly increase the amount of feeling and aliveness they experience. Many can feel their sexual energy running through all their cells. Experiencing this for myself and in others has been a revelation, such a joy, a reclaiming of our more authentic nature.

I teach people not to hold their breath during orgasm, as the holding cuts off the natural extension of their ecstasy. We breathe all the way down into the pelvis and expand rather than contract. To women, I encourage a pelvic-floor push out—as if having a baby—which can prolong the orgasm. Through these teachings, I've learned to have orgasms and over time have different kinds of orgasms: energy or breath orgasms, multiple orgasms, and G-spot orgasms with inner nectar (amrita) flowing abundantly.[2] These methods demonstrate the limitations of the belief that a peak orgasm is all there is. Clients who had almost lost hope often find they can consciously learn to have an orgasm.

As a Tantrika I often lead ceremonies and rituals. Once at a party given by artists, I decorated the room, greeted the guests costumed in full Tantric regalia, and Tai-Chi-danced in shelled-out half watermelons full of bite-sized fruits. Playfully and sensually, I fed the fruits into many mouths. Later I face-painted the participants and finally danced erotically in the main course on elegant platters. I loved raising people's sexual energy; and though I'd met many men who wanted to take me home afterward, I chose to go home alone as my sexual energy had been channeled into the sensual orchestration.

Another high-priestess experience included my skills as an erotic environmentalist. I spent the afternoon bringing in flowers and

---

[2] [Ed.] *Female ejaculation* would be the Western sexological term for "flowing amrita."

beautiful bedsheets, arranging the altar, setting up candles, cutting up fruits, and in the evening guiding a consummation ceremony. A just-married couple had invited eight close friends to share their special consummation evening. The ceremony started with an outdoor fire where songs and prayers were shared. Then a temple priest washed their feet. As they entered the beautified yurt, they were smudged and undressed. Sensual, easy-access attire awaited their choosing. We toasted with champagne and fruits, and then the wedding couple went to their rose-petaled bed in the center of the yurt. I guided the others to focus their love and energy toward the newlyweds for the next half hour. We chanted and danced free-form around the couple's bed, then visualized our energies merging with the couple in the center as they joined in physical and spiritual union. It was a wondrous, erotic, tribal celebration—a unique and auspicious wedding consummation.

For individuals and couples, a typical Tantra training session begins with Tantric philosophy, specifically about the chakras,[3] their location, function, and some ways to purify them. Then I teach a few breathing practices that can release stress and eventually create openness. The next session deals with any specific sexual problem or interests the client might have (e.g., premature ejaculation) and appropriate exercises are given. Then I introduce the ceremonial elements of how to use fire, earth, air, and water to create a conducive space for prolonged and sensual lovemaking. Next, there are partner exercises that create specific energy flows between hearts, minds, or erotic zones. The idea is to open the chakras and sense organs so that the depth and subtle energies of each person are ignited and a full exchange of this energy can happen with each other.

---

3 [Ed.] *Chakras*, a Sanskrit term, refers to spinning energetic vortexes in the human subtle-energy field. Their functioning is often associated with physical and emotional health.

Very few of my sessions in Tantra have been overtly sexual. The few that were, were mostly with virgins after three or four Tantra sessions (similar to what a sex surrogate might do).

Richard was a twenty-four-year-old American male whom my boyfriend and I shared a house with one summer on the island of Ibiza in Spain. One morning, after having a date the night before, he shared that he didn't know what to do with women. He said, "I'm a virgin, I don't know how to kiss, pet, or make love. I've never even seen a nude woman's body....Will you teach me how to go about all those things?"

I thought for a moment and said, "I suppose so, but let me see if it's OK with my boyfriend." He felt compassionate for our roommate and with little thought agreed. Thus, I had my first experience as an "initiatress" in the full-fledged sense.

In India during intermission at a tabla drum concert, another young man, an Indian of nineteen, approached me. He came straight out and asked me to teach him how to make love to a woman. At that point, he didn't know I was a Tantra teacher. I didn't respond then, but he came and sat with me during the second half of the concert. He was forward and persistent, and finally I told him he could come for a few Tantra sessions and we'd see. He was sincere and receptive, so on his fourth session, I initiated him with a sexual rite of passage. The day before I left for the West, he came with a bouquet of flowers and gratefulness in his eyes and heart. Here I was, an American, teaching an Indian the art of Tantra yoga, which had originated in his culture some five thousand years ago. Today not only is Tantra mostly a lost art in India, but most of the people are very sexually repressed and ignorant about Tantra.

My clients come from all walks of life. They want to integrate their sexual energy and become better lovers. They want to feel more pleasure and more aliveness. An Australian businessman whose wife had lost interest in sex wanted to know any techniques that might revive her interest. A black yoga instructor wanted to know how to run that yogic energy with his lover. A New Zealand woman who had been shunned in her upper-class surroundings for her erotic energy wanted to open consciously to that energy and receive healing around it. A divorced landscaper with three children wanted to have more relationship and sex skills before looking for a new partner. A man whose lover had left him for a more artistic man wanted to release the grief and sadness in his heart. A thirty-seven-year-old foxy woman who had had a traumatic first sexual experience at age eighteen wanted to open her pelvis and become orgasmic. She had faked all but two or three orgasms in the past twenty years.

Working with people all over the world, I've gained much experience and compassion for the human predicament and the human capacity to experience happiness. To others I want to hold out the possibility of self-healing, for I myself come from a dysfunctional family of alcoholic parents, wherein my own needs were seldom, if ever, met. Learning that I had a right to ask for what I wanted and needed sexually was a challenge.

I'm very thankful that my work contributes to the quality of my and other people's lives. The grace and openness I've gained from working intimately with people enrich me. I can be at ease with them whether they're crying, experiencing revelations, raging at their parents, being in bliss, or having an orgasm. I've gained a lot from helping people breathe through to their own sexuality and juiciness.

For the opportunity to teach in other cultures and the adventures I've had, I'm grateful. For having freedom in my working schedule and the chance to choose my own hours, I'm thankful. With these blessings have come many lessons. I've had to learn a lot about trust and flexibility as there were hardly ever guarantees about fees or number of students. I've learned how to make boundaries, especially when clients wanted to get overtly sexual during or after a session when I wasn't interested or available. I've learned about the necessity for creating a safer space for this work. I've learned how I need to purify once a year from my clients' energies by fasting and being at the sea and with nature.

For me, being a Tantrika has been the *path of fire*.

SHELL FREYE

❦

THE GROUP-SEX HOSTESS

Introduction to

SHELL FREYE

"Love to love ya, baby, love to love ya, baby, love to love ya, baby, love to love ya, baby..." It was the American sex mantra, recorded on a popular disco album repeated for hours in the background while I gave massages at Shell & Barry's group-sex parties.

In the waterbed within inches of my portable massage table were usually one or two nude couples playing, enjoying anything from fondling to having full blow-out orgasms with bombs bursting in air. Juicy vaginas and throbbing penises were abundant next door in the "group room." This was where one person might be sucking on the toes of a person, who might be giving head to another person, who might be sucking the breasts of another person, who might be balling somebody else's brains out, and on and on. No one ever asked me for a sexual massage—all the sex one could ever want was plentifully available.

This was a private home where three nights a week Shell became a high priestess greeting couples at the entrance to her temple. Worshippers were gathering to celebrate the union of heaven and earth; to commune physically, emotionally, spiritually; to share food, dance, hot-water bathing, and consensual sex.

Actually very few participants in a swingers' party, the usual term for such a male-female couples' event, would ever think of the parties as spiritual ceremonies. Most swingers appear nonreligious. How could a couple be in an open-sex lifestyle and think of themselves as spiritual when for centuries priests and preachers, claiming to be God's personal emissaries, have raised their Bibles high into the air and screamed to the top of their lungs that sex is inherently sinful, that sex shall be for procreation only, that adulterers and those who partake in the pleasures of the flesh *shall* burn in hell!

There was no exit, no alternative to the scarlet letter, the adulterous *A* imprinted deeply in the collective mind-set—until *the pill.* Overnight, women's options to choose their own sexual destiny were greatly expanded, if not always in individual practice, at least in the collective consciousness. For many women and men, this was the beginning of a sensual/sexual revolution.

Shell's parties were a significant part of that revolution in the San Francisco Bay Area in the '70s. At the time, little was written about the sex-positive nature of some Goddess cultures and the transformative role of the temple priestess/sacred prostitute. Looking back now through the eyes of the recent Goddess literature, I think of Shell's group-sex parties as temple ceremonies celebrating one of the high holy mysteries: sexual energy. For some of us who attended, we began to realize that there was more than just a whole lot of shakin' going on at those parties. We explored, we learned, and we grew.

Shell, the soul of the parties, grew profoundly. Deeply immersed—eating, sleeping, working, living—in her temple where wave after wave after wave of orgasmic moans, arousing pheromones, and visions of rapture permeated every pore, she was able to step, sometimes stumble, sometimes soar, outside both the mainstream culture and the swinger subculture to discover the mystical energetic dance where sexual passion—transformed—is a catalyst to our spiritual Self.

Osho, a Tantric sage from India, once said, "Sex—never repress it! Never be against it. Rather, go deep into it with great clarity, with great love. Go like an explorer....Sex is just the beginning, not the end. But if you miss the beginning, you will miss the end also."

Through twenty years of sex-party hostessing, Shell has explored sex deeply. Sex was the beginning for her. Now she is fully grounded in her sexuality, physically resembling some of the Paleolithic statuettes of the Goddess. Now she is a teacher with a mystic's vision of sexual energy. And what she discovered at the center of her sexuality and her dance of energy—what has always been there, at the beginning and the end—is her heart. This is where she teaches from, where she hostesses from, where she dances from. Her heart is what makes her sex sacred.

THE GROUP-SEX HOSTESS

by

Shell Freye

with Carol Heller

It was a humid Brooklyn summer day in 1965 and I was twenty-one. My husband Barry and I were lying in bed looking at postage stamp-sized photographs of couples in a little swingers' magazine called *Continental Spectator*. With the windows open, a floor fan blowing hot air across my thighs, looking at the tiny photographs, I realized I was getting aroused, but I didn't understand why.

We had been married for approximately six months, and my husband asked me, "How would you like to meet some of these couples?" Being very naive, I said OK, on one hand knowing the purpose of meeting would be to "swap" partners and have sex, on the other hand not really believing that we would actually do it. We answered some ads and placed a very simple one of our own to which several people responded.

Having had no prior experience with "swapping" as it was called then, I remember creating an elaborate fantasy about what this first meeting would be like; there would be soft music in the background, a stranger would sweep me off my feet, and take me into his curtained boudoir, just like in the movies. In reality, when our first encounter happened, not only was there nothing sensual about it, it wasn't even exciting. It was cold, unromantic, and boring. Intrigued by my fantasy of what might occur, I decided to keep pursuing swinging.

Our first encounters at some of the other couples' homes were such a letdown that I couldn't participate. After an hour or so of socializing, I would make up some excuse about being tired or not feeling well so that we could leave gracefully. This led Barry and me to the decision to have people come to our apartment so I would feel more comfortable in our own atmosphere.

When we first started entertaining, we decided to invent verbal code words so I could let Barry know if I was interested in engaging in sex with the couple. He was to ask, "Did you feed the cats?" If I wasn't interested I was supposed to say, "No, I didn't." If I was interested, I would answer, "Yes, I did," at which time Barry would make a suggestion that we get more comfortable and I would turn down the lights and put on some music. At our first tryout of the code words, I was flustered and I answered, "Maybe, I'm not sure." He looked at me as if I was crazy and said, "Let's go to the kitchen and check the cat's bowl." We used the code successfully after a while, and I started to feel a little more adventurous.

Eventually we branched out to events and private parties that were held in penthouses, apartments, the spa in a hotel basement, and large homes outside of New York City. We discovered there were clubs where we could meet with other couples for future "dates."

One of the first private parties we were invited to was held in the basement spa of a well-known hotel in Manhattan. I remember entering the lobby with my husband and several couples, wondering if any of the people in the lobby knew where we were going and what we would be doing. The swinging scene was still new to me, and I had been fantasizing about this event for days. We all crowded together in the elevator and descended in silence. When the doors opened, and we stepped out, the first thing I remember seeing was the steam rising off the heated pool. The effect of the lights reflecting off the low ceiling made it seem as if the subdued sounds of women and men making love were coming from the reflection. As my eyes grew accustomed to the dim lighting, I could see bodies and shadows moving in the water. It was all very exciting, and for a moment the possibility existed that the evening might turn out like my fantasy.

The elevator doors closed, and the host approached us, introduced himself, and began showing us the facilities. He led us down a long dark hallway to the steam room, where he suddenly flung open the door and the steam poured out, hitting my body like a wave. Gradually, as the vapors cleared, I could see different levels in the room with bodies on all of them, moving and melting in the steam. However, as the steam settled I noticed that, unlike my fantasy, there were mostly men in the room with only a few women.

As our guided tour continued we walked around the pool past a man who was lying on a bench while a woman performed oral sex on him as she was being entered from behind by another man. It appeared so harsh and mechanical that I couldn't tell if any of them were enjoying themselves. It turned me off, and I wanted to get out of there. However, still hoping for that quality of connection and "magic" that so far was missing, we stayed a little longer.

Somewhere in the back of my mind I had created a detailed image of what group sex would look like. I know now that it was strongly influenced by the art of the masters that I had been exposed to as a child growing up in the San Francisco Bay Area. My parents, who were theater people, had always been very loving and supportive; and being an only child, I was immersed in their Bohemian lifestyle. Poetry readings, art shows, gallery openings, jazz, and dance performances were commonplace events that shaped my perception of life as well as my appreciation for colors, shapes, and textures. If I had seen women and men touching sensuously in my early swinging experiences, it would have been what I expected. However, the reality was, "Slam, bam, thank you, ma'am," with mostly no "thank you"!

One particular environment that really excited me was the nightclub, where you could either meet at the tables or on the dance floor. At one nightclub all the tables were equipped with telephones that had large numbers attached to the back of the phone. You could call other couples at their tables and arrange to meet them by inviting them to your table for a drink. We would talk for a while, and then I'd usually ask the man to dance with me. The music, low, sensual lighting, and dancing equated to foreplay for me. Since I had been a student of modern dance from the age of fifteen, dancing and moving my body allowed me to express myself. Dancing seemed to be a way that I could feel my own sexual energy. I found it easier to connect with a dancing partner because when we are dancing, we can feel each other's rhythm. This, I quickly realized, was what had been missing in all the other environments. I began to call it "connecting" with the other person.

Like most young people in their twenties, I was willing to be adventurous when it came to exploring my sexuality. However, many of the swingers in those early days in New York would leer at me or try to interact and initiate sex with little or no foreplay. My recollection is that the swinging scene was fast, similar to the pace of the city, and many times insensitive to the need that many women and men had for tenderness. If I was to continue in the swinging scene, I was determined that in my environment this would not be true.

After three years of experimenting with sex on the East Coast, particularly New York City, we moved to Oakland, California, my hometown. This was 1968, and we joined the Sexual Freedom League. In California everything was freer and more open than it was in New York, but even here I had a reputation for being very particular. Most of the time I did not participate because I was not comfortable. Similar to the way it often felt in New York—cold, hard, and fast—the level of intimacy didn't seem to matter to most of the men. While many women did join in, it seemed to be mainly the men who participated most often. I still had a difficult time feeling sensual or relaxed enough to take off my clothes and jump in. Little did I know that I would make up for lost time later.

One of the first parties we attended in California made me realize that I could set up a party environment and do it better. I knew I was a terrific hostess, and my penchant for paying attention to details such as music, soft lighting, soft colors, and sensuous food would create an intimate atmosphere that could arouse me so that I would feel secure enough to want to join in the fun. In my own environment I could create a place where sensuality and promiscuity could flourish. We discussed it and quickly saw we needed to move to a bigger place that could be set up specifically for large parties.

We found a house to rent in Berkeley and put an advertisement in the *Berkeley Barb* for "Swingers Friday Night Socials." When couples called in response to the ad, we would interview them over the phone and then invite them to the Friday evenings. If we liked them, we would personally hand them invitations to come back on Saturday nights for our "swinging parties." This was our way of screening a number of couples at one time. It also allowed the other couples to meet. What we were looking for were couples with a good relationship who took good care of themselves physically and who were, hopefully, compatible with the others.

There was a very large response to the ad, and our parties grew from five couples to around twenty-five to forty couples within one year. The living room was for getting acquainted with other couples, listening to music, having a drink, or getting something to eat. Because of my past experiences of walking into a room where several people were "getting it on" in one corner, while several others sat in another corner looking very uncomfortable, I wanted the living room to be neutral, so I decided that no sex would be allowed there. In the past I had felt pressure to join in and later regretted doing so; therefore, I wanted people to have the option of choosing to participate or not.

After two years at the house, in my continuing personal search to enhance my sexuality, I decided to incorporate an experience that I had had in a workshop on sensory awareness. I felt that this encounter would enhance the parties, so I used what I had learned and tailored it to a sexual setting. Adding a personal touch of my own, I included nudity. I wanted the swingers to be able to be sexual in an easier, more natural way. By prearranged agreement, the evening would unfold with couples being blindfolded as soon as they entered the foyer. In silence they were led to the living room where they sat in a circle with the other couples until everyone had arrived.

My first step would be to put on some special, relaxing music. The next step would be to teach them how to do certain breathing techniques. From there they began touching their own faces, which led to touching their partners' faces, becoming aware of the warmth, the texture of the skin, the way the hair felt, and how unique the sense of touch became without the sense of sight. They would then stand up and come closer together as a group to begin exploring someone else's face, which led to touching their shoulders and arms. Next I would guide them through a way of showing the other person how they wanted to be touched. Sometimes it was two women or two men touching each other's arms. Some felt comfortable and some did not. The idea was to become aware of different sensations while touching, sometimes applying pressure, sometimes using a lighter touch. Eventually the entire group began to undress one another. Once they were undressed they sat down, and I would bring in platters of fresh fruit for them to identify by smell and taste. Then slowly they would start to feed each other. After a few minutes of this, I would ask them to remove their blindfolds so they could see whom they had been feeding. Usually everyone would end up laughing and hugging, and the party would be on its way.

Because of the size of this first house, I wasn't able to achieve the nightclub atmosphere that I wanted. The decor we had chosen was sensual and intimate, but I could see in my mind's eye what I wanted to create, and this house had limitations. About this time fate stepped in. The landlord sent us a letter that our house was being put on the market for sale, and we were offered first option to buy. Knowing it was too small for our growing business, we declined and had ten days to vacate and find another house.

Within one day we found the house that would become the setting for parties for the next twenty-plus years. My father came with me to see the house. I had explained to him that our business was a social club, a place where like-minded couples came to meet, dance, and get to know each other in the setting of a private home rather than a bar. The subject of sex was never mentioned to him and he chose not to ask any questions even though I had lots of mattresses and very little furniture to speak of. Because of his experience with running and owning a nightclub, he was excited to help his daughter, who was seemingly following in his footsteps. Dad convinced me the house had a good flow to it. And I felt enough support from him that I asked him for a loan for the down payment.

My mother, also, was very accepting of the social club format we had explained to her. She never directly asked what my specific involvement would be, choosing instead to believe that Barry and I were just the host and hostess. If she had asked, I felt close enough to her and my father that I would have told them we were swingers, but it never came up. What she did say was: "You're serving food. Are you going to charge anything? Can I help you with the decorating?" She and my father and several friends helped us move in and decorate, so that within ten days we had our grand opening.

There were two ways someone could come to the party. One was by answering our ad. The other was by personal recommendation from friends who had been to the party. After we briefly interviewed the couple on the phone, they could make a reservation for one of the upcoming evenings. They would arrive in our typically quiet neighborhood, park their car, and walk down the path to our door.

This was reportedly the most difficult part for some new swingers: the walk from the car to the house. Over the years many reported the anxiety they experienced sitting in the parked car, unable to open the car door. I wasn't able to alleviate these feelings until they stepped through my front door.

I personally greeted them at the front door. Once the door closed behind them, their reality shifted to mine. The sweet fragrance of incense filled the air. As their eyes adjusted to the soft lighting, I explained the layout of the house to them.

It was 1972, and I wanted the decor to be different from that of a home setting. I chose low, comfortable seating with lots of pillows in the living room, instead of couches or chairs. This was on the main floor, to the left of the entryway after coming in the front door. The room was lit by the glow from the fireplace, and indirect, pink lighting bounced off the curve of the ceiling. This room was for socializing only, as it had been in our previous house.

At the far end of the room a curved archway framed the dining room, where the hardwood floor made a perfect dance floor. Replacing the regular bulbs in the crystal chandelier with blue bulbs gave a remarkable reflective quality to people's skin as they danced. A large glass window separated the dance floor from the buffet area. This added to the effect of being "on display" as you danced. You were able to see your reflection as you moved to the rhythm of the music, and you were seen by others.

From the side of the dance floor, you entered the kitchen. Off the kitchen a doorway led to the sun porch, which we had decorated with an African motif. This was where a sumptuous buffet was served. Downstairs in the finished basement, black lights accented the decor. There was a group area in one room, and in another room we draped gauze curtains around several single beds, giving the illusion of privacy for those who had voyeur and exhibition fantasies.

One of the favorite places in the house was the circular staircase that led to the top floor. Standing at the bottom of the stairs, you were able to enjoy the parade of bodies moving up and down the steps.

On the top floor, we had created a haremlike atmosphere in the upstairs group room. The walls were covered with fabric that was accented with peacock feathers. Mounds of pillows covered the beds. Containers of massage lotion, boxes of tissues, and vibrators, for those who wished to indulge, were placed strategically around the room.

The master bedroom, as in our previous house, was reserved for special private encounters for Barry or myself. A third bedroom on the same floor was designed as a more private area, and the beds were separated by ceiling-to-floor curtains draped around them.

My concern was always for women to be comfortable so that they could explore their sexual possibilities. I had too many memories of being uneasy in my earlier swinging encounters, and I promised myself that I would not allow that to happen to anyone in my house. Past experiences also told me that if a woman felt at ease, her partner would too. I wanted this place to be an arena where all could be relaxed the minute they walked through the door. The soft lights, the colors of the fabrics, as well as the paint on the walls were all purposely chosen for a specific ambiance to create different moods that allowed people to relax and explore.

Always searching for new ways to cultivate my personal growth, I became a certified masseuse. This led me to explore a new career as a sex surrogate. Because of my years of experience with swinging and the variety of sexual partners, I was a natural as a surrogate. I soon discovered I needed to have formal training in order to facilitate the client's process.

The Institute for Advanced Study of Human Sexuality, in San Francisco, provided the clinical training that was missing. Entering a three-year program that gave me a very well-rounded education, I became the first certified sexologist in the state of California.

I learned that I had the potential to give more than just sex—there was also energy. *Energy* is my word for the translucent, multicolored web that connects us all, that holds and embraces us throughout all our actions in life, regardless of any belief systems we might have. In my search for knowledge I was fortunate to discover a teacher who helped me experience the sacred nature of energy.

Every time I learned from him something new about moving energy within my body, I would practice it at the weekend parties.

What he taught me was how to consciously open my heart and my pelvis by doing breathing and visualization practices. After most of the people arrived and started to socialize, I would begin dancing with a partner or with the others dancing around me. Beginning with an inhalation, I would visualize a band of energy or light spiraling up my body from the base of my spine. I would feel the motion moving around me and then inside of me, continuing to move up and around my heart. It then circulated down, in and around my pelvis. Actually seeing the band of light moving outward from my body, I visualized it surrounding those I was dancing with, encasing them in a spiral of light. I could see it moving into their hearts, circulating down through their bodies into the pelvis and returning to me. Keeping them in the spiral I would then envelop another and another, until the whole room felt like their bodies were connected to mine, moving with the same rhythmical motions.

People would dance for a while and slowly begin to drift away to other parts of the house, in couples or groups of three or more. As others took their places on the dance floor, I would begin to weave them into the energy as well. At first I wasn't too sure of what, if anything, was happening. As a test to see if what I did really had occurred, I would do the breathing and visualization practices in reverse, pulling my energy inward and seeing myself sealed off from the others. The party would become flat.

One evening while I was practicing, a masseur named Ray Stubbs came to the party, having been invited to give three hours of ten-minute massages for those lucky enough to get on his list for the evening. We had met at a lecture on sensual touch several months before, and I recall experiencing a special quality of balance within him. Afterward I had a private session with him, which led me to ask if he would be interested in teaching some classes at the parties. This was to be the beginning of a new adventure for both of us, and especially for the swingers. It opened them up to an invisible energy they were feeling but knew very little about.

My desire was to share some of this knowledge with the swingers. With me as his partner, special evenings were offered with Ray leading a group of couples through erotic massage techniques. With twenty couples packed in the room, we would work together, introducing feathers, fur gloves, lotions, scented oils, and strawberries. We introduced different ways of kissing, stroking, exploring, touching. On those evenings the mirrors on the ceiling in the group room were misty with steam. I could feel the anticipation of each person in the room growing with every caress. These evenings would bring a special magic to the entire house, even to those who did not participate. Calling it "holding the field," I included everyone in the house by energetically weaving them into my field and one another's, never forgetting the people downstairs while these instructional evenings were going on.

On occasion a new couple would arrive and the woman, sometimes the man, would be experiencing anxiety similar to mine when I was first starting out. Noticing their discomfort, I would encourage them to sign up for a massage. Including them in this way would allow them to feel as if they were participating, and many times being touched would help them to relax enough to join in.

Over the years we introduced other aspects of sexuality to the swingers. There were women-only evenings set aside for women who wanted to explore their sexuality with another woman, sometimes for the first time. These evenings differed from the regular parties because no men were present. Feeling a common bond, we all danced together; it was softer, more sensual, and very relaxed. At these parties women seemed to dress in fabrics that were more flowing, revealing, and erotic. On these nights, as I practiced weaving the energies, it gave me the feeling of being at a temple performing a sacred ritual. Sometimes erotic massage techniques were taught, but mostly we would have great conversations on very intimate issues that related to our swinging experiences. Even those who had never been with a woman before reported feeling very at ease and natural. I can still recall sitting in the living room listening to the hum of the vibrators and the sweet sound of orgasm echoing down the staircase from the group room above.

Saturday night erotic entertainment could be anything from belly dancing to stripping contests to lingerie parties to wearing exotic costumes to a lecture and demonstration on sadomasochism. Both men and women participated in all of these events.

As I continued to explore and expand my sexual fantasies, I would incorporate what I learned into the parties. The films I saw, the erotic literature I read, the workshops I attended, the times I went to the bisexual evenings at the Sutro Baths, all of these would stimulate my eroticism and I would in turn improve the environment of the party house. My fantasy life was rich and fulfilling, which in turn influenced my life. Knowing that everyone had fantasies and probably nowhere to act on them, I provided a place that gave permission and encouraged exploration.

The joy I received from providing a beautiful and sensuous place for people to expand their tactile, visual, and sensual awareness was, and continues to be, very rewarding for me. When I stand at the doorway of the group rooms watching bodies intertwining, I become immersed in the pure pleasure of the moment—it is an ecstatic *be here now*. As we accumulate experiences, whether as a participant or an observer, these moments become embedded in our memory. Keeping this in mind, I have tried to set the stage and provide an environment where positive sexual fantasies are not only encouraged but happen many times. I am not advising anyone to go to a swingers' party, but I am encouraging continuous communication, exploration, and tenderness. When a couple shares such intimate experiences, it brings them closer and can help build a deeper relationship.

In my twenty-plus years of involvement with swinging, the fact that all these people continue coming to the parties fascinates me. Swingers are ordinary people from every walk of life. They are bankers, executives, store clerks, cab drivers, teachers, to name a few. They all have one thing in common: they are open about sex. It doesn't mean that outside of the swinging environment they're promiscuous, because most of them are not. As a rule you won't find them in bars trying to pick people up, won't find them hustling, won't find them seeking affairs. Many of the couples I know have solid, long-term marriages, children, even grandchildren.

Many couples who attend the parties now choose to engage in sex only with their partners. They can be in any of the different private areas or the group rooms, but they stay together and allow the sexual energy and visual delights to stimulate them. This is their way of practicing safe sex in this era of AIDS. Other couples still have multiple partners, but latex gloves, dental dams, and especially condoms are used regularly.

After so many years of being open and available, several years ago I felt I needed to take a break from the swinging scene. I have continued working in the field of sexuality as a lecturer and as a counselor for couples and individuals. The energy work I learned has become invaluable and I incorporate it into my counseling sessions.

While I was taking my break, Barry continued to run the parties and just this year I have returned to them. We still remain close friends although we divorced several years ago. At this point in my life, my role at the parties has changed. I have returned as a hostess and have discovered that I don't have to physically have sex with anyone, and the energy still prevails. I still enjoy being around sexually open-minded people. The group always changes, but many of the couples that were there years ago still participate, having remained close friends with one another.

Looking back at the changes that have taken place, not only in my life but also in the lives of the people I have connected with, what has remained constant is the energy. Not only do I continue to learn about myself as I teach, but my abilities to direct and "play" with energies are stronger now than when I first learned to open up my heart to connect with others.

Over the years, I have touched and been touched in many ways by many people. Each one has helped me be who I am today. For this, I am deeply grateful. My hope is that I have touched them as deeply as they have touched me.

BETTY DODSON

❦

THE ARTIST

Introduction to

BETTY DODSON

Betty Dodson is a wild woman. While described in the Introduction as charging the barricades with a vibrator in one hand and her *Liberating Masturbation* book in the other hand, Betty is neither out of control nor deranged nor savage. She is wild in the sense of undomesticated; she lives outside many of society's normative restrictions.

In *Women Who Run With the Wolves*, Clarissa Pinkola Estés, Ph.D., describes the Wild Woman archetype. Comparing the wildness of wolves and women, Estés writes: "both have been hounded, harassed, and falsely imputed to be devouring and devious, overly aggressive....They have been the targets of those who would clean up the wilds as well as the wildish environs of the psyche, extincting the instinctual, and leaving no trace of it behind" (p. 4).

Betty Dodson is a wolf in the wilderness, howling at the moon, reminding us of our primal sexual nature. Her drawings and paintings depict women and men naked and sexual and inherently beautiful, making love with themselves and others. Her books, videos, lectures, and workshops extol us to reclaim our birthright as vibrant orgasmic beings, a birthright stolen and hidden from us by religious and political fanaticism.

An artist seeing the natural, unmuzzled, ungirdled, unreigned sexual beings that we all are, Betty has been in the vanguard of sexual liberation in the second half of the twentieth century. For this, she, as she describes in her chapter, has been labeled pornographer and whore. Rather than retreating in defeat, she reclaimed her personal power by embracing the terms, reframing the negative epithet into a positive call to arms: "When the ultimate degradation, 'Whore!' was hurled at me, I welcomed that label too. 'Yes, I'm a whore, a sacred prostitute, an ancient temple priestess who serves the goddess of love.'"

By reclaiming her own power and teaching others what she has learned, she empowers others. Betty, who recently received her Ph.D. in human sexuality, puts her ass on the line; and though at times a weary, embattled general, she holds true to her inner truths. Her vision, simply, is freedom for herself and for others: "freedom to think, freedom to fantasize, freedom to imagine the unimaginable—in short, the freedom to be creative."

THE ARTIST

by

Betty Dodson

When I first began thinking about teaching sex to women, I knew it had to be experiential. As an art student, I had learned by doing. In fact, every time I learned something new that involved my body—a sport or the latest dance steps—I didn't just sit in a classroom thinking and talking about how to make the moves. Actually, sex, sports, and dance had a lot in common: rhythm, movement, form, content, and aesthetics. But how on earth could I teach sex by doing sex, short of staging sex parties? That would restrict the number of interested women, and I was aiming for every feminist in America.

That was my dilemma in the early seventies when I was bicoastal and the women's movement was no longer on the launching pad waiting for liftoff. In New York City and San Francisco thousands of us were orbiting the planet with ideas about how to achieve more equality between women and men. This energy was contagious because everything seemed possible. And each woman's history became her agenda for change once we learned that the personal is political.

After thoughtful analysis of my own sex history and subsequent sex experiences in the late '60s, I came to the conclusion that sexuality was as critical as economics in women's quest for equality. All of my cherished romantic illusions had either mystified my lack of orgasm or aggrandized my dependent orgasms as I searched for financial security through love and marriage. As long as women remained blinded by love and bound by an invisible sexual and financial double standard, feminism would never pose any real threat to our present authoritarian system.

Once committed to the women's movement, it didn't take me long to discover that my idea of liberating masturbation was too shocking for most feminists. Few were interested in becoming responsible for creating their own orgasms, alone or with a partner. Most women wanted just a little bit of freedom: equal pay, child care, access to the political process. But when it came to sex, they still wanted to find Mr. or Ms. Right who'd provide them with love, orgasms, and security *forever*.

At first I was devastated and hurt, and then I became furious. Turning my anger into energy, I resolved to go it alone—the artist's fierce stance of individualism. The conservative, mainstream feminists could fight the good fight for the Equal Rights Amendment while I would storm the barricades waving my banner for the Equal Orgasm Amendment.

In 1973 I began running Physical and Sexual Consciousness Raising Groups, which turned into the Sexuality Seminars that I still run to this day. Since I was an artist, not a therapist, I felt free to break all the rules, especially to avoid the role of being an "expert" who knows all the answers. First-person sharing of our sexual experiences seemed the best way to learn about sex. I shared what I'd learned about sex from several sources: my own sex history, reading extensively about sex, drawing sex, having three one-woman exhibitions of erotic art where I talked to hundreds of people about their sex lives, and gathering a wealth of firsthand sexual experience by participating in group-sex parties.

My first approach to teaching was demonstrating manual sex, showing the use of electric massagers and dildos, and encouraging everyone to develop a repertoire of sexual fantasies as a way to focus their minds on sex instead of drifting into running a grocery list. I also acted out a range of orgasms from mild to intense, giving women in the groups a visual image that was worth a thousand words. Later they practiced masturbating at home with follow-up discussions in the next group session.

Within several years, the workshops developed a basic pattern. The two main subjects were healing our body and genital imagery, and learning the basis of orgasmic release through masturbation. The only requirement for attending a group was agreeing to nudity. We all benefited from seeing natural bodies instead of constantly comparing ourselves to fashion models and centerfold nudes. There was no doubt in my mind that selflove[1] started with loving our physical selves.

Originating with my own self-therapy, I'd already developed a method for confronting women's negative genital imagery. In 1965,

[1] [Ed.] Betty uses *selflove* and *selfsexuality* rather than the standard hyphenated versions of the words through all of her writings.

shortly after my divorce, a lover had shown me magazine photos of women exposing their genitals because I'd confessed mine were deformed. Until that moment, I'd thought my inner lips had been stretched from childhood masturbation! To share this healing experience with other women, I created a slide show of one hundred beautiful color photographs of friends' genitals that premiered at the historic 1973 Women's Sexuality Conference sponsored by the National Organization for Women (NOW). The presentation was titled "Creating an Aesthetic for the Female Genitals." Afterward, I was given a standing ovation that sent shock waves of compassion and excitement through me.

Providing positive genital imagery became an essential ingredient of the workshops. At first, showing the slides to each group was sufficient until I realized that looking at ourselves directly would have an even more profound impact. One by one, starting with me, we took turns under a spotlight in front of a freestanding mirror, displaying the exquisite shapes and colors of our vulvas. My fine art background was perfect for showing each woman how "to see" her unique beauty, shape, and form. We were also getting an important lesson in comparative anatomy by viewing a range of genital appearances. This single process transformed a multitude of women's sex lives by dispelling myths and filling in information about our clitorises, vaginal lips, strange little bumps and tags at the vaginal opening, secretions, the urethra, the PC muscle, different colorations, scars from episiotomies, and the interesting range of pubic hair.

The "Genital Show and Tell" breakthrough gave me the courage to propose to one group that we actually share orgasms in the workshop. To my amazement, they all said yes! In those early days, the group masturbation was informal, with everyone lying down, using their electric massagers, doing their own thing. Most of the women kept their eyes closed, but they could hear the sounds of breathing with a few audible orgasms, and they could sense the energy in the room.

Eventually, I got the inspiration to lead the group in a guided masturbation celebration. Sounding like an enthusiastic gym teacher, I started with the group standing in the circle with our massagers on and our eyes wide open. Sometimes I was a rock star playing my massager like a bass guitar; other times I was a top sergeant barking out a cadence. There was always great humor and bawdy comments with lots of healing laughter. We were more outrageous than I ever expected! For the first thirty minutes, I led the group through different sexual positions: standing, kneeling, doggie style, and lying down with different leg positions. We varied our pelvic thrusting while breathing out loud to increase sexual pleasure. I showed them how to do slow pelvic rocking with a fast massager, or the reverse, fast pelvic movements with a stationary massager. We practiced slow, sensual penetration with cucumbers or zucchinis and coordinated our breathing with tightening the PC muscle while rocking our hips forward and back. What I said, I did, modeling each concept with a live, visual image.

Our masturbation celebration ended with an erotic recess. Everyone was shown how to keep going after her first orgasm by putting her hand over her clitoris to soften the vibrations until the hypersensitivity passes. In moments she could continue into another sexual buildup. Having many orgasms was easier and more natural than most expected, and pushing at our sexual boundaries was exhilarating with group support. Most women were only spending ten to twenty minutes on selfloving, and here we were, masturbating together for nearly two hours and having a great time.

Teaching sex by doing sex was the most logical thing in the world. Everyone got to see a range of sexual arousal and orgasmic responses. Right before our eyes we witnessed the huge variation in women's sexual patterns. Some women had many little orgasms with quick buildups in between. Others took thirty minutes to an hour to have one big orgasm, and there were a few who could have several fairly big orgasms, each with a visible buildup. There were also those women who were having little spasms that they did not label "orgasm" because of their expectations. Unable to identify the beginning of their orgasmic response cycle, they couldn't create more sexual pleasure.

Clearly, masturbation was the key for sexual growth. It gave each woman a chance to focus totally on herself instead of being concerned about pleasing a partner. She could take as long as she wished, try all sorts of different things, and experiment with creating new fantasies. From selflove and sexual self-knowledge, I reasoned, healthier and happier relationships would naturally follow. And for women who wanted to be on their own for a while, they could be their own lovers.

It took several years, but after I got over my concerns and fears of teaching sex with this logical but unheard-of method, I began having some of my best orgasms in the workshops. The combination of playing teacher, being a voyeur of the erotic sights, exhibiting my sexuality in a group, and getting paid to masturbate to orgasm was hedonistic heaven.

The concept of teaching sex by doing sex will be perceived by many as a kind of prostitution. The minute a woman accepts money or favors for sex, she is flirting with the world's oldest profession. Women (and men) who have sex with clients under the supervision of a therapist are called sex surrogates, practitioners of the most effective way to help clients learn about sex. Again, many people will consider this to be another form of prostitution, even though the surrogate has received training and must submit reports to the therapist. On the other hand, if a wife receives money or a new fur coat for sexual favors from her husband, it's viewed as normal. A sexworker[2] friend liked to point out that marriage was legalized prostitution with one difference: a wife sold her body permanently, while a sexworker only rented hers. Most women will smile knowingly at this kind of remark because we sense the primal connection between sex and money, though it's seldom discussed.

If I'm getting paid to have orgasms with women who are also having orgasms, does that make me a sexworker? Is masturbating with my students considered "having sex" with them? Does watching another person masturbate count as "having sex"? What about viewing sex for research purposes as Masters and Johnson did? How does anyone do legitimate sex research if she "follows all the rules"? Denying educators and researchers the right to participate in a range of sexual activities results in a lack of valid and complete information for textbooks. Those researchers who have participated must lie about their sexual experiences to remain acceptable. Too many sex teachers are ineffectual because they don't know enough about real, live sex. They have not had sufficient experience to even identify their own sexual problems.

Most of our contemporary images of sex are based on what we see in the movies or on television. Often we get kissing as a stand-in for sex. The alternative is lovers frantically ripping off each other's clothes with mouths glued together until they fall onto a bed, still half dressed. We seldom get to see scenes of slow, sensuous sex. Instead, we're bombarded with images of sexual urgency, desperate grabbing with mouth mauling, and compulsive kissing. When passion equals urgency, sex becomes a rush to the finish line.

For those of us who rent X-rated videos, images of sex aren't much better. To create more drama, most porn directors encourage faked female orgasms with screaming and bucking. Male orgasm is

---

2   [Ed.] *Sexworker* is a recently evolved term referring to women and men who provide for a fee a sexual service/entertainment, such as nude dancing, sexual intercourse, sexual massage, and phone sex.

represented with ejaculations flying through the air, often landing on some part of a woman's body. Nothing like a big glob of jism pooling in the corner of a heavily massacred eye to turn most women off porn. Maybe coming on a woman's face is revenge for all the times we've said, "Careful, don't mess up my makeup." Or from some men's point of view, perhaps it's a symbolic way of making a woman more of a participant in the sexual action instead of remaining a passive sleeping beauty.

Some fine scripts for X-rated movies could be based on people's wild ideas about what takes place in my workshops. One time after explaining how I taught sex by doing sex, my listener imagined me dashing around the room giving each woman an orgasm. One of my married students' husband was convinced that on the second day I'd bring in the men to fuck the women. His wife sweetly explained, "There will be no men, darling, just our zucchinis." One student's fantasy of my workshop was being made love to by a group of lesbians, while I made suggestions to improve each one's technique. I must admit that some of these fantasies were so intriguing, I used them for my own private masturbation. However, having people drift into a sexual fantasy while I was talking about the reality of my teaching got to be very frustrating.

"Someday, I'll make a video of the workshops," I often thought as I looked around the room and saw the glorious images of sex. When I turned sixty, after describing my workshops a million times to prospective participants, reporters, TV talk show hosts, teachers, students, and strangers at parties, I finally decided to make a videotape that shows what I'd been doing all those years.

At every turn, the problems seemed insurmountable. How could I get a group of women together who would be comfortable with this kind of sexual exposure? The minute a camera enters the room, the experience would be altered. Was there a way to light the group during the masturbation celebration that would hide our faces?

Maybe the women could wear wigs, or sexy masks. It went like that from the beginning, but in the end, my biggest problem was myself.

How did I feel about more public exposure? Wasn't it enough that I'd written about my personal sex life for thousands of people to read? Wasn't it enough that I'd shared orgasms with my workshop women for twenty years? I was having a monumental struggle with the idea of being nude at my age, displaying my genitals, and mass marketing my orgasm for all the world to see. My long-departed mother's voice kept ringing in my ears, "Betty Ann, you always go too far." Clearly, one of the biggest challenges of my life was at hand.

The entire production was handled by my partner Samantha and me. The shooting was the easy part. To my amazement, all the women were ready to "come out." The tough part was the endless hours we spent in the editing room with me looking at my sixty-year-old body. I, "the Queen of Selflove and Body Acceptance," sat there day after day passing critical judgment on how I looked. I wanted less of me, more of the women, and I sounded like a parrot who kept repeating, "Cut, cut, cut."

After weeks of carrying on like that, one day Samantha turned to me and asked, "Could you please get over yourself so we can move along?" Whammo! I got it and shut the fuck up. Not that I didn't continue to agonize over "looking good," but not speaking it was the beginning of letting it go. About halfway through the editing, one day I was suddenly outside myself, viewing the tape with detachment. As I watched this gray-haired, motherly woman with her granny glasses, I became entranced. She was right-on, she was talking straight, she was the bravest of generals on the front lines with her troops, she was doing what she was saying, she was walking her talk. A genuine admiration for her welled up inside me, and I began to actually like my older self. The final outcome was a one-hour video titled *Selfloving: Video Portrait of a Women's Sexuality Seminar*.

After twenty years of hearing myself and listening to women share their sex lives, I found that one of our most consistent problems is the constant power struggle going on inside each of us: good girl vs. bad girl. The morality that's been shoved down our throats from religion, government, school, and the family has conditioned us to be divided within ourselves. I no longer have any illusions that masturbating to orgasm will eliminate this conflict, but having an orgasm with ourselves is at least a moment of getting in touch with our bodies and senses that just might support individual choice over all those conditioned responses.

Another barrier to becoming fully sexual is most women's insistence on having romantic love and passionate sex with some mythical, perfect lover. By constantly being focused on finding fulfillment "out there," we never have a chance to look within, to develop the ability to fantasize, or to create new erotic images that would consistently charge our sexual desire and arousal. Instead we are stuck with our repetitious dreams of romance.

People use the word *romance* to mean many things. However, my dictionary said it quite well: *A fictitious tale of wonderful and extraordinary events, characterized by much imagination and idealization.* If this were a definition of sexual fantasy, it would work. But confusing "fictitious tales" with reality causes some serious problems. When lovers turn into ordinary persons with blemishes and flaws, when the burden of trying endlessly to sustain sexual passion through increasingly artificial means finally fails, we fall out of love, only to repeat the pattern again.

These romantic images feed our notion of what sex *should* be like. As a teenager, I remember longing for a penis inside my vagina with my "true love," knowing the experience would produce an orgasm that would be far and beyond anything I'd ever experienced from masturbation, including all the orgasms from handjobs with my teenage boyfriend. Ironically, in my second year of marriage, I was secretly masturbating to memories of those hot, high-school handjobs.

Contrary to much of the available romantic literature, an orgasm is not always a grand mal seizure, especially when a woman is first learning about sex—alone, with a new lover, or with her husband. A good example was Alice, a fifty-two-year-old woman who came to see me privately. At our first session she said, "If I could have the 'big O' every time my husband and I made love, I'd be happy." Occasionally she was having what she called "small orgasms" with her partner of thirty years. Every Friday night they had sex, and when a little orgasm came along, Alice would think, "Oh, that's nothing." Unable to build upon her existing sexual response, she kept beating herself up with her sexual expectations. It was similar to wanting to go from walking ten blocks to running a ten-mile marathon with nothing in between.

I recommended Alice start practicing orgasm with herself on a regular basis. If she could learn to give herself those same "little comes," she could focus on intensifying her experiences of orgasm gradually. Since she dislikes electric massagers, I suggested she do manual stimulation while I watched. The room was not that warm, so Alice only took off her skirt and panties. Sitting along side of her, I had her oil her genitals, and then asked her to stimulate her clitoris. She had a heavy-handed movement that was quite clumsy. It reminded me of watching a small child tying a shoelace for the first time. Even simple, basic skills require learning how to make the moves.

Wearing a lubricated latex glove, I touched her with light pressure, using different movements that I verbalized. "I'm making small circles with one finger; this is two fingers above, below, and alongside your clitoris. Now I'm using my whole hand to stimulate your clitoris more indirectly." After doing herself by imitating me, she said it did feel good, but then she lost interest and all sensation in about five minutes. Her homework was to masturbate whenever she felt like it, but to make sure she cradled her genitals in one hand every night before she went to sleep. This was a comforting gesture that would help her to get used to touching her "private parts," as she called them.

On our second session she was happy to report her marital sex was definitely improving. A new appreciation for her husband's handjobs was now producing orgasm for her most of the time, and she was beginning to get pleasant sensations when she touched her genitals. Although she had been unable to give herself an orgasm, with time, practice, and patience, I'm sure she'll succeed. In the meantime, she's thoroughly enjoying the Friday-night orgasms with her husband.

The idea of touching a client is severely frowned upon in most therapeutic circles. Perhaps the reason for this was to protect clients from sexual advances by therapists. While this might present a problem for some, I personally have never felt an overt sexual desire in a teaching context. For me, the laying on of hands is an integral part of any healing process. Rather than calling myself a "therapist," I see myself more as an "orgasm coach" who helps clients change their behavior. That doesn't mean I don't include some standard therapeutic processes, such as listening to a person's problems, verbal probing, and gentle guidance that will lead to insights. We need to take advantage of every possible approach in helping people to discover sexual pleasure.

My individual sessions have also included coaching a woman through her first extramarital affair after twenty-five years of monogamy. She had no information about male sexuality except what she had learned from being with her husband, and she had no idea how to tell her new lover what turned her on. I urged her to include her electric massager with her new lover since it was the only way she could orgasm consistently. The affair only lasted a few months, but it had a wonderful effect on her marriage. She gained the courage to use her massager with her husband, and she started having orgasms with him for the first time.

Another private client, a young woman in her early thirties who had never had an orgasm, actually had one during our first session after getting some basic sex information. June had been using the massager by bearing down and relying only on pressure for her sexual buildup. After a while, she had to stop because the massager was creating pain instead of pleasure. We experimented with different layers of a washcloth between her and the massager to control the intensity of stimulation. She liked the cloth folded once. Then I showed her how to put the massager to the side, above, but not *directly* on her clitoris for any extended period of time and to keep it in motion. I paced her breathing with the sound of my own, reminding her to keep her pelvis rocking gently forward and back. Next we added the PC muscle. As she rocked forward, she squeezed the muscle, and coming back, she let it go and relaxed. Then she tried several different dildos. Picking the one she liked, I asked her to explore the sensations inside her vagina by pressing the dildo in different directions. She preferred a downward position. Finally, I suggested combining all of the elements: moving the massager, rocking her hips, slowly moving the dildo in and out while she squeezed her PC muscle, then releasing it, along with pacing her breathing. After about fifteen minutes, she had her first orgasm, much to our mutual delight. June left with her self-esteem soaring.

One woman in her forties came for a session, wanting to know if she was "doing it right" and where on a scale of one-to-ten would I grade her sexual response. After watching her masturbate by hand, with a massager, and also using a dildo for penetration, I assured her she was doing great! She had a nice orgasm, paid me, and left feeling elated knowing she was a "ten" according to "an expert." Part of knowing who we are sexually comes from other people's feedback, but she'd never been able to talk with anyone about her sex life, especially masturbation.

Another example of the absence of sexual self-knowledge was a shy woman who didn't feel comfortable taking a group, so she booked a private session. She said her orgasms were fine, but she worried a lot about whether or not she was normal "down there." Using the same process I did in the workshops, I sat alongside her while we looked into the mirror together. Her genitals were beautiful, with long inner lips that looked like lovely drapery with a perky clit at the top. Her relief showed on her face, and she smiled from ear to ear when I told her she had one of my favorite styles of genitals, "Baroque." This simple reassurance made her feel more complete.

Afterward, I wondered what her mother had thought when she diapered and washed her baby daughter's genitals with those abundant inner lips? My own experience of being imprinted with a non-verbal message was verified in a conversation with my mother when I was in my forties. In my first book, *Liberating Masturbation*, I'd included fifteen drawings of women's genital portraits, and also told the story of my imagined genital deformity. After reading my book, my mother admitted she'd been concerned about my extended inner lips when I was a baby, always wondering if I was "normal." I held that nonverbal message until I was thirty-five years old.

Most sex educators agree that our first sexual messages are non-verbal. Maybe it goes all the way back to the circumstances under which we were conceived. When we were growing inside our mothers, what did it feel like when they had an orgasm? Did our fathers speak to us during the nine months of gestation? What would it be like if mothers had orgasms during the birthing process while fathers provided clitoral stimulation? I've had several workshop women describe giving birth in this manner, and each time, the image inspired every woman in the room.

Sexual inspiration is an important aspect of the workshops. During the guided masturbation celebration, women are getting some erotic images to play back the next time they masturbate. I always encourage everyone to explore their minds for images or ideas that turn them on, including reading erotic literature or watching X-rated videos. In most workshops, after we have dinner, we come back to my apartment and I put on some sex videos for them to watch. They see blowjobs, cum shots, anal and vaginal fucking, gay handjobs, and lesbian oral sex. There is no baby raping, no dismemberment, no violence—just pictures of sex.

Currently, pornography is being blamed for rape, incest, wife battering, date rape, child abuse, and sexual harassment of women in the workplace. These aberrations stem from *sexual repression*, not graphic pictures of human sexuality. While it's true some pornography is low on aesthetics, that just makes it bad art. We have to remember that the crusade to end pornography is really an attack on our first amendment rights and an effort to control our sexual freedom. Freedom is not free. We need to speak out against religious bigots who demand we all have monogamous marital sex for procreation, and anti-porn feminists who are intent on preserving romantic illusions by demanding their lovers be faithful, including no more beating off with *Playboy* and *Penthouse*!

Although most of my work has been around female sexuality, I have done a few workshops and some private counseling with men. Some middle-aged men have come to see me just for the thrill of sharing masturbation with an interested woman who won't be judgmental. Most of the older men have problems with erections, and they're convinced their sex lives are over unless I can give them some magic trick to restore their *potency*. Yes, you guessed it, masturbation to the rescue.

Using the same techniques I teach women, I have them use an electric massager, assuring them they can have an orgasm without a hard-on. At first, most men complain about not liking the sensation of an "electrical appliance," but I ignore their complaint and keep talking. "Just keep breathing, rock your pelvis, squeeze the PC, and fantasize I'm Marilyn Monroe." Usually I can see the moment they let go of their resistance, get into the good sensations, and finally come all over the "electrical appliance" with a soft-on. They admit the orgasm felt great, but want to know how can they have sex with a woman without a hard-on. I list the ways they can be good lovers: massage, manual sex, oral sex, either partner strapping on a dildo for vaginal or anal sex, using other sex toys for penetration, using one massager for two, and sharing masturbation where both people have their own massagers—to name a few.

The other big problem for men is ejaculating too soon, becoming flaccid, and believing in the arbitrary *thirty-minute refractory period* that ends the sexual exchange. One workshop woman said, "My husband has a thirty-day refractory period." I believe the lack of erections and premature ejaculation is the counterpart of women not coming at all. These men are "preorgasmic," although we never use that term when we're talking about male sexuality. The solution for both preorgasmic women and men in basically the same: masturbate, and train your body to respond to sexual stimulation. Men can learn to control the urge to ejaculate by contracting their PC muscle and squeezing the penile glands before they reach the point of no return. The erection will subside a bit, but with continued stimulation, it comes back for more. Men also need to be encouraged to use lots of sensuous massage oil when they masturbate, especially if they are circumcised.

In my opinion, sexual ignorance keeps us from making the connection between the pain of circumcision and sexual dysfunction in men. We know our bodies hold the memory of pain in the muscles and connective tissue. Such memories would affect the penis as well. Circumcision is an unnecessary and barbaric surgical procedure

that's performed without anesthesia. Doctors act as though the foreskin is nothing but a piece of worthless flesh, but it's perfectly
designed to protect the delicate penile glands. All the sensitive nerve
endings in the foreskin greatly enhance masturbation and intercourse. Some sex researchers believe that up to 40 percent of penile
sensitivity is lost when the foreskin is removed. In every workshop,
I appeal to all the mothers not to fall for the "cleanliness rap" as a
reason to remove a baby's foreskin. Every mother can clean her
baby's penis until he is old enough to be shown how to wash himself. We don't cut off our ears because they're difficult to clean.

The concept that we armor our bodies with fat or rigid
muscles to protect ourselves from pain originated with Wilhelm
Reich. He believed the natural flow of sexual energy leading to repeated experiences of orgasmic pleasure was the opposite of the authoritarian personality with an armored body and a rigid mind dedicated to sustaining control and power over others. He talked about
the absolute necessity of having orgasms on a regular basis in order
to maintain mental health and personal happiness. Orgasm was more
than a biological function of procreation or the side effect of casual
pleasure: "It is the very center of human experience and ultimately
determines the happiness of the human race."

Fleeing the rise of fascism in Germany, Reich came to the USA
only to become a victim of America's fascism. His theories challenged
our entire social and political system. When Reich extended his theories to define the function of the orgasm as the Life Energy, it was to be
his undoing. Giving sex the status of a cosmic healing force flew in the
face of our Judeo-Christian doctrine, which permitted marital sex for
the purpose of procreation only. Not only did the religious establishment rise up in arms, but the full fury of the Food and Drug Adminis-
tration and the American Medical Association was unleashed. Reich
was put in the Federal Penitentiary at Lewisburg, where he died
November 3, 1957, a day of infamy for our entire justice system.

Teaching sex by doing sex hasn't always been an erotic bowl of cherries. Aware I was treading on dangerous ground, I learned to walk softly. Always mindful of the defenders of the status quo, I knew religious fanatics, right-wing politicians, and anti-sex feminists were all capable of violence. However, most of the attacks on me and my work came in the form of name-calling that was meant to degrade me personally or to demean my words and art.

One of the first labels hurled at me was "pornographer." Lacking any experience with the word, I was angry and hurt. "How could anyone find my beautiful drawings pornographic?" But soon I learned that name-calling was at the heart of all censorship. The real issue at stake was freedom to think, freedom to fantasize, freedom to imagine the unimaginable—in short, the freedom to be creative. My healing came when I stopped defending myself and embraced the label. "Yes, I'm a feminist pornographer who believes in first amendment rights and artistic freedom." Next came the pejorative hiss, "lesbian!" which was supposed to intimidate me back into passive female conformity. "Yes, I'm a lesbian feminist who loves both women and men." When the ultimate degradation, "Whore!" was hurled at me, I welcomed that label too. "Yes, I'm a whore, a sacred prostitute, an ancient temple priestess who serves the goddess of love." Taking on all the labels allowed me to claim my power.

My sexual evolution has been an integral part of my spiritual growth. Once I understood that masturbation was a meditation on selflove, my sexuality and spirituality grew closer together. When I think about my other spiritual practices, I put art near the top of the list. Drawing was a beautiful meditation, and mastering the nude was an excellent discipline. The creative process and developing a sense for aesthetics—the search for beauty, its sources, its forms, and its effects—will always be a profound spiritual consideration for me.

Although I came from the Bible Belt in Wichita, Kansas, my parents were not religious people. Mother thought the Bible was a collection of fairy tales, and that only ignorant people believed it was the word of God. My dad was an atheist. With no religious pressure, I naturally wanted to join a church. So Mother took me to a Methodist church to be baptized at twelve. After a few months of boring Sunday School and a brief stint of singing in the choir, I got over wanting to belong to an organized religion. But I kept searching for something outside myself to give life a special meaning.

My spiritual quest has been very eclectic because I explored each new teacher, group, or process that intrigued me. First I was into psychiatry and group therapy. Next it was General Semantics and non-Aristotelian thought, followed by *A New Model of the Universe* by Ouspensky. That led to studying the teachings of Gurdjieff, which was basically a form of esoteric Christianity for a chosen few. After that I got involved with the twelve-step programs that opened their doors to everyone who had a desire to stop using their drug of choice. I began studying and practicing yoga. I took Tantra workshops. For a while I worshipped group sex as the highest Tantra ritual. I learned Transcendental Meditation. Becoming a vegetarian, I turned health into a religion. I went on retreats, I fasted, I got colonics. I became a feminist and turned that into a religion. There were many psychic readings where I learned about my guardian angels, spirit guides, and past lives. I studied metaphysics. I got Rolfed, rebirthed, and had foot reflexology. My horoscope was done; I used the Tarot cards and then the I Ching. I worshipped the goddess and made up my own rituals. I joined a lesbian SM[3] support

---

3   [Ed.] *SM* and *S&M* are terms referring to forms of erotic expression usually employing the consensual playing of *dominant* and *submissive* roles along with activities resulting in intense sensations which a nonparticipant might label *pain. Bondage and discipline,* also consensual, are often involved in such erotic play. *SM,* the term, derives from the concept in psychopathology known as *sadomasochism,* though SM as consensual erotic play would not usually be pathological. Ironically, SM advocates' use of the term *SM* functions as a playful "topping" of naive SM opponents.

group. I did Smokenders three times. I took the Forum and some of their follow-up seminars, and a couple of years ago, I did a week-long Avatar seminar. Although in many ways I'm a doubting Thomas, I love to read about ETs, Light Beings, Pleiadians, and flying saucers. I continue to practice my sexual meditation with masturbation.

Every teacher, each discipline, and all of these groups taught me something about myself—a steppingstone along a winding path. But the struggle between "turning my life over to a power outside myself" and "being committed to questioning all authority" always bailed me out. My need to be an individual on my own terms would pull me back into the mundane world to grapple once more with my divided self: good girl vs. bad girl.

Maybe it was because my initials spelled B.A.D. that I tried so hard to be good. But in the end, the juiciest bit of wisdom I gleaned was that I was both good and bad in an imperfect society. As I continue along my spiritual path, one thing is sure: I know the path will never remain the same.

Every time we follow gurus or teachers we adore, they become authority figures and we end up surrendering our power to them. Although I might be addicted to being adored, I have never wanted to perpetuate that kind of authoritarian control, especially over women who took my workshops. I used to call myself "a one-night-stand guru." With each passing year, I realize more and more the importance of designing a method of teaching that required women to take only one, or maybe two, workshops. After that, there was nothing to join and no way to see me on an ongoing basis. The antithesis of sexual freedom would be creating thousands of little Bettys who were all having orgasms just like me.

While the Eastern-guru craze has somewhat subsided, we now have a rash of Americans teaching sex under the labels of Tantra and Taoist sex practices. Most of the information about Tantra sex is speculative at best because it had an oral tradition that was taught

to the same old "chosen few," who then become "spiritually enlightened." I have no problem with the idea of people teaching rituals
that treat sex as a form of meditation, that encourage breathing techniques, or that promote better communication skills between partners. But the use of the word *Tantra* confuses more than it explains
by mystifying sex. Tantric teachers are being puritanical when they
use Hindu words to talk about sex and body parts. We need to
diffuse the English words so people can speak about sex more
comfortably.

While I personally believe my sexuality and spirituality are
closely connected, I don't want to go overboard by turning sex into
a religious practice. And I certainly don't want all of my orgasms to
be sacred, ecstatic, ritualized communions with some divine purpose. There are times I just want a *quickie* with a scuzzy fantasy of
being tied down and fucked by a sadistic scoutmaster and his
entire Boy Scout troop.

Now that we are in the '90s, I'm still perceived by some people
as "weird" to be sure, but I have also been acknowledged by many
wonderful people who respect my simple message: "Selfsexuality
is the ongoing love affair that each of us has with ourselves throughout our lifetime." Teaching masturbation by masturbating has kept
me fairly honest, not that I don't still lie to myself occasionally, but
when you see your teacher *playing with herself*, it's difficult to turn
her into someone who is more than human or larger than life.

Given the current political power trip of the Religious Coali-
tion, with its agenda to control the way people worship, live, and
love, it's surprising that I have received such a small amount of hate
mail. Instead, the file folders marked "love letters" fills up several
times each year. I've heard from educators, clergy, doctors, lawyers,
lesbians, mothers, housewives, soldiers, prisoners, nurses, healers,
therapists, nuns, priests, bankers, artists, executives, writers, enter-
tainers, and other folks who didn't identify themselves. It's very

much like the women who take my groups: a cross section of America in all its glorious diversity. Their common interest is a desire to know more about human sexuality, especially selfsexuality.

I have always been excited by the possibility of change for every woman who has taken a workshop. Sometimes the change takes place before my eyes; other times I get the feedback later on. Getting a first orgasm is thrilling. Some younger women with new lovers have told me they're beginning to explore what turns them both on with a more open dialogue about sex. Married women have said that sharing their sexual self-knowledge with their husbands has charged a flagging sex life. Mothers have talked with me about not interfering with their children's natural sexual exploration with masturbation. More women are dispelling myths about romantic love. They're no longer confusing good sex with love. Some are questioning the ideal of monogamy when they know it rarely exists. Couples who do choose to be monogamous are agreeing to a single standard. Women are also taking a hard look at jealousy and possessiveness as a healthy way to express a loving posture.

Today I believe sex energy is not only the life force, but also the source of all creativity. Each orgasm is a precious moment of joy. Sex quiets the mind, deep breathing brings oxygen into the bloodstream, the heart is exercised as it pumps blood through the veins, hormones and endorphins are released, the skin sweats, muscular tension is heightened and then drained, followed by deep relaxation and a sense of well-being with feelings of contentment through an intimate connection with ourselves or another person. As we awaken our bodies through the senses, we awaken our minds to the knowledge that all living things are connected—on Earth and throughout the vast universe.

CAROLYN ELDERBERRY

❦

THE MASSEUSE

Introduction to

CAROLYN ELDERBERRY

When I answered, Juliet Carr was on the phone. She quickly said, "Carolyn has just been busted!"

"Those pigs!" I responded. I immediately flew into my rage. "Those macho assholes are afraid to confront the crack dealers toting automatic rifles. Erotic masseuses don't shoot back. What a waste of taxpayer money—these are consenting adults!" It took me a while to calm down.

As it turned out, Carolyn had been the calmest one of us all. She had remained centered, even after the vice squad's onslaught that was to leave her eye badly bruised and blackened when the kicked-in door of her home slammed against her face. When she had chosen to do her full-body massage therapy, she knew that someday she might be arrested on prostitution charges for doing what is popularly referred to as "sensual massage," sometimes as "erotic massage" or "sexual massage."

Carolyn does a lot more than total-body touch. She has a bachelor's degree in psychology, and from the San Francisco Theological Seminary she received a master's degree in the area of ethics. For her master's degree project, she developed and then later taught in her church a sex-positive sex education program for early teens and their parents (*sex-positive* meaning that abstinence is one of many options and that a god's wrath is never threatened as a motivating factor). She was trained and then volunteered on sex information hot lines, spending hundreds of hours answering on the telephone the sex questions of young, middle-aged, and senior people of all sexual orientations and persuasions. Carolyn has also been trained as a sex surrogate and is certified in massage therapy. Moreover, she identifies as Christian and is an ordained lay minister in her church.

My sense of Carolyn Elderberry is that she feels morally bound to serve humankind and to serve from a heart space. So when the vice squad rushed into her home with their guns drawn and she was completely nude with a badly bruised face, she was confronted with the moment of truth: could she walk her love-all-of-humanity talk and turn the other cheek?

She told me later that it was during the experience of being arrested and being stuck in a cold holding cell (where guards refused her even a single blanket to keep warm) that something opened up inside and without fear, anger, resentment, or regret she realized that she was on the right path, doing truly righteous work, having a meaningful impact on people's lives doing her full-body/mind massage work.

Nine months after the arrest the charges were dropped due to "a lack of evidence." It was then, committed to her values, Carolyn decided to go to the office of the undercover vice squad officer who had taken off his clothes and received her almost two-hour session. There, turning the other cheek, she explained to the officer that she would continue to do what she had been doing in her sessions before the arrest. She went on to explain the real nature of her work and her intent in facilitating her clients to have more meaningful lives.

The chapter that follows is that story.

THE MASSEUSE

by

Carolyn Elderberry

WILLING TO BE HONEST?

Want to Improve Life?
I'd like to help you feel good
about yourself & improve your
important relationships. Hands-on
massage/bodywork & caring talk…

My work involves talk, touch, eye contact, presence. The work begins when the client reads the advertisement above, telephones, and listens to a two-and-one-half-minute message. If he's interested (most of my clients are males), at the end of my message I join the line and we talk.

The phone conversation may be quite short because the caller has not understood my message. He may be attracted to stay on the line because I sound friendly and I take a personal interest in my work. Sometimes I suggest a course of action, reading, or professional consultation as being more appropriate than coming to see me. I may invite the person to call in the future after he has done some of the suggested exploration.

Some callers may not be familiar with the mystical, spiritual, or holistic concepts I speak of in my message, but they are responsive to what they have heard so far and want to know and understand more. What feels "right" for me is the way the prospective client and I understand the implications between the lines of words. The client may immediately demonstrate that we are like-minded by saying he is looking for an integrative experience and the possibility of enhancing and expanding other areas of his life; he is not merely looking for an interlude of sensuality or a titillating sexual experience.

In the early years of my work I didn't screen out clients looking for brief sexual interludes. I did emphasize the aspects of being a teacher, counselor, confidant. I also spoke long enough on the phone to determine that this prospect was not crude in his sexual attitudes. I preferred education and refinement, but I took long enough to not turn working-class men away merely on that basis. I found many such men to be quite sensitive to relationship and sexuality. Since I offered to teach, an outgrowth of my history as a school teacher and of my training as a sexual surrogate, it felt appropriate to see men wanting to learn about sex and technique.

It took me some time to learn that the men I was talking with frequently misunderstood me because they thought I was speaking euphemistically.

A good example is a man who very nearly did not become a client. I greeted Habib at the door and showed him into my massage room and invited him to sit down. He began to look uncomfortable and began stammering.

"You use a table?"

"Yes, of course I use a table for massage. Why?"

"Um…uh…I don't want a massage."

"Hm…wasn't I quite clear on the phone that what I do is massage? It's full body and sensual and erotic."

"Yes, you were clear, but…"

"But what?"

"Um…well…I, uh, um…"

"You thought you could talk me into 'sex' once you were here?"

"Um, yeah."

"I'm sorry. I thought I was perfectly clear."

"You were, you were. But it's not what I want. Not today. Maybe some day I will and I'll call you."

I smiled and showed him to the door. He gave me an apologetic look and repeated that he was sorry.

The next day Habib called to apologize. He realized he had taken a couple of hours out of my workday and that he should not have left when I had not misled him what to expect. Before hanging up, he promised to call in the future and make an appointment for a massage.

A few weeks later when Habib arrived, he sat on the sofa while I massaged his feet. He's a hard-working immigrant with a large family. He treats others with respect and really felt badly that, previously, he had not kept his disappointment to himself and completed our transaction. I reassured him that I was fine with his conduct and appreciated the responsibility he took toward me and my time. We continued to get to know one another and feel comfortable. I asked him to stand and began undressing him. We hugged and...he came. Needless to say, he felt some embarrassment. I reassured him and encouraged him onto the table for some massage. He reluctantly agreed, but after only five or ten minutes he was restless and indicated it was time to leave.

Upon his departure, we both felt we had shown respect to one another and felt better about the prior misunderstanding. He said he would call again, but I rather doubted it. He was a tense person, hard driving, focused on work and activity—definitely not a massage aficionado.

As I evolved in my work and became clearer about the criteria I used in the screening conversation, I would see fewer clients who were, in fact, simply shopping around for sexual variety. I wanted ongoing client relationships so I would be able to grow while also helping my clients. Profound encounters *should* change us. I was not seeking shallow or superficial experience in my work. If that was what I wanted, it was available in the sexual play world. My intent was to validate, to support individuals in feeling good about themselves and their healthy sexuality. I was willing to spend a lot of time through conversation to motivate my clients to grasp and appreciate a broader perspective of sexuality than they had considered.

To my surprise, Habib did call me, and became a quite frequent client. I learned much about his family and his powerful drive to provide well for them. He had all his children enrolled in parochial schools; he was devoted to his wife, and his fooling around was...well, just fooling around.

Several more times he came before getting on the table. I'd keep reassuring him and teasing him about his active imagination that led him to such quick orgasms and emphasized that learning to relax and receive massage would also help him to delay orgasm. I secretly wondered about his wife, wondering if he always came so quickly. When I asked about his wife, he told me that she enjoyed sex and was very willing and accommodating. What he didn't tell me was that he was to become a father again. Six months after meeting, he proudly told me of his son's birth. That gave me a better understanding of the frequency of his visits to me.

For a number of subsequent visits, Habib could contain his pleasure and get onto the table, but he couldn't last once I touched his buttocks. I worked with him to relax and receive my touch. I taught him to tell me, in time, when he needed me to stop the touching so his excitement could subside.

At the end of the first year of visits, he had worked up to staying for half the regular appointment time: thirty minutes. Gradually he would relax more and stay longer. It was a real triumph the first time he arrived and said, "Wow, I really need a massage," and was able to wait until late in the appointment to experience orgasm.

We've been seeing each other seven years now, and he is quite a different man from the one I met. We share information about our real lives, our feelings and hopes and frustrations. Habib was the first Palestinian I had met. I had avoided knowing Middle Eastern men because I was sure they were all male chauvinists and very macho. Habib has shown me that masculine pride can be expressed through a profound responsibility to family and community. Within the parameters of the professional relationship we have, we are friends who have grown and enriched each other. Frequently Habib comes to enjoy a full hour of massage, to physically relax and let go tension, to feel turned on—yet will have me avoid his genitals so he can take all the energy home to his wife!

Now, before I agree to an appointment, I must have a sense that the client will be receptive to my work, will be willing to talk honestly and is already making some changes in his life, working toward more balance and better physical conditioning. Since my work is about health, I find it counterproductive to accept clients who engage in an unhealthy lifestyle, and I accept only those who have either stopped smoking or are seriously in the process of doing so.

In the initial call I always ask about personal life and want to know about marriage and children, if that is his situation. Those callers who are not comfortable may hang up or tell me this is not their interest, so we end the conversation. Other times I speak very directly to their issues and guide them toward working it out with their partner or working on themselves to discover their motives and reasoning rather than seeing me; usually I can't know if what I said did any good, but once in a while a person calls back to thank me. Sometimes I point out that I am the wrong person for them and thank them for their call. If the caller is comfortable talking about his personal life, and especially if he welcomes this conversation, we make an appointment.

When the client arrives, I show him into the massage room. The light is soft; the colors, warm. He sits on a sofa, I on the floor, and I remove his shoes and socks while we begin talking. Obviously we are assessing each other at this point. I'm helping him to settle in and become comfortable. I'm also getting a lot of information about his body as I massage his feet. Soft music is playing in the background.

After about twenty minutes we stand and I begin to undress him. It's a caring gesture, one with which many men are awkward at first but generally come to enjoy very much. I remove my own shirt and skirt. I'm in lingerie, he's in undershorts. Frequently I ask if he'd like a hug. I notice his ease or unease with hugging. I also notice the tension in his back and shoulders as I run my hands over these areas and usually make a comment. Then I remove his shorts and invite him to lie face down on the table.

I begin massaging—long, slow strokes from the top of the back down onto the buttocks, returning with a light touch. I begin to move over different areas, assessing the tension, letting my hands find their own way. I maintain maximum skin contact, including my forearms as much as possible, allowing my body to lean into the table when I'm at the sides. I'm mindful how adults rarely receive touching and how nurturing a gentle and warm touch is. While I'm practiced in clinical therapeutic massage and my massage is indeed therapeutic, my strokes, rather than being simply clinical, are an extension of myself and my caring for this human being on my table.

I want the message from my hands, my being with him, to be: "Relax, you're loved, valued, appreciated." I want cells, sinew, bone, muscle to receive this message. I don't fight tension in the body. I enter the tension to coax it to release itself and open to the flow of energy. I allow my body to come into tune with the body I'm encountering. I become aligned with him. I don't consciously think what to do. I don't "see" what needs to be done. My hands find their way. I become linked in a caring way with him. Without awareness, at first, I begin to make sounds as I work, soothing, purring sounds, like cooing with a baby. Bit by bit, the client eases, relaxes. Frequently I hear soft (and sometimes not so soft) snoring. The body is getting much needed rest, release from care and worry and activity. I feel the body, the tissue, softening. Sometimes I support the tension, taking over with my hands and body the superfluous work of the muscles, and gradually they relax and let go. A sense of well-being suffuses the client.

Generally I massage down the back, over the buttocks, move to the feet, and then up the legs. If there is little tension in the shoulders and neck, I will probably find very tense legs. I knead those calves, warming them with gentle friction. As the tightness leaves, I lengthen the strokes. Sliding up the inside of the thigh, I lift the flesh softly as I move outward just under the buttock and press in on the sit bones, treating this neglected area to gentle but firm pressure. Finally I begin at the feet and make long strokes to connect all of the body, sliding down the arm and back down the leg. After several of these strokes, I return to the head, massage the scalp and neck, then give more strokes on the back and shoulders. Next I give light, feathery strokes in large sweeps over the entire backside. This "wakens" the skin and brings a delicious tingling into consciousness. Now it's time for him to slowly turn over onto his back.

At the head of the table, I slide my hands under his shoulders, push the pads of my fingers upward, and let gravity help work out the shoulder tension. I begin kneading the neck and shoulder area, gently moving the head in different directions, loosening, soothing, encouraging release of tension. Sometimes I massage the face now; other times I move to the torso, pressing smoothly and evenly, coaxing the flesh to soften and give up any tension. Pressing in a circular movement, I move down the torso. I begin moving both hands together, clockwise, over the abdomen. Now I slide my hands down the sides of the body. When they reach the table, my fingers slide under the torso, then outward and upward, gravity helping again. Moving up the torso, I include the arms, then back to the torso, sliding and gliding, moving onto the pubis, making small circles, sliding my fingers along the crease where the leg joins the torso, continuing down the inside of the thigh with the flat of my hand, up over the thigh, my hand lingering where I find tightness, stroking, gliding, kneading…continuous motion, cradling, nurturing this body in my hands. Back up the legs, the flat of my hands massage the inside of the thighs, turning as I lift the scrotum, supporting it in my palms and bringing my hands around and up the shaft of the penis, now back down and onto the torso. I may move up to the head again, without lifting my hands off the body, include the neck, and give long strokes over the torso, crossing a hand above the penis, then moving my hand backward and under the scrotum, lifting, stroking, treating the testicles gently, lovingly, as a wonderful part of this body, lightly lifting off, faintly touching the penis as I return to the torso. I repeat these slow, gliding strokes, sometimes moving onto his legs, sliding my hands up his thighs, under the scrotum, lifting, stroking, gliding....

What I am doing is not a "handjob" or "jerk-off." By including the genitals, I'm telling the body it is whole and wholesome. Too often, the male genitals have been disparaged. The client's genitals have rarely been admired and appreciated by women.

Though I avoid focus on the genitals because that would only reinforce the notion that sex equals genitals, I do not ignore the genitals. Rather, I am demonstrating to my client that it is the whole body that is sexual. I encourage him to become aware of all his sensations, his toes, his fingertips. When he begins to hold his breath and focus on his genital sensation, I encourage him to keep breathing, to keep the energy channels open, in effect to learn to experience more pleasure more intensely than he has. This is a process of learning how to prolong and heighten sexual responsiveness.

I continue this process, including his nipples, the pleasure of which is a very great surprise to some. I've removed my bra; and as I lean in toward the table, I can also add more skin contact by brushing his body with my breasts. On some strokes I will lightly drag my nails across his skin, adding more intense tingling sensations. Sometime during this part of the massage most clients will experience orgasm and ejaculation.

Men who become ongoing clients will, over time, learn to allow more and more sensations to flood their bodies. They may learn to reach orgasmic pleasure without ejaculation, allowing the feelings to gently subside and then build again...and again. This type of response was once thought to be experienced only by women, but men can learn and enjoy it as well. After he ejaculates or begins to allow the intense feelings to cool, I will use a slightly firmer stroke beginning at his genitals, pulling the energy, the sensations, down his legs, up his torso, out the fingertips and toe tips. Then I move to the head of the table and gently massage the head and neck while he floats in bliss, feeling so relaxed.

Currently my appointments are an hour and a half, so there is no need to rush and there is usually plenty of time for the resolution (resting) phase. Finally, I signal that the time is up, perhaps gently kissing him on the forehead, or whispering something softly in his ear, or laying my hand over his heart, feeling and sharing the energy.

Usually, when clients first visit me, they become aroused quite quickly. Sometimes they come before they've been touched (other than the feet); other times, like Habib, as soon as they are touched anywhere on the body; and some with the first touch of their genitals. Over time, these men learn to relax and experience the rest of their bodies. They learn to enjoy the massage.

Few men realize that they had had an erection during their first twenty-four hours of life. I first learned this observing my own son when the pediatrician was examining him. Anyone who has watched infants and toddlers unclothed knows that erections come and go and are not directly connected to what we, as adults, call sexual stimulation. Teenage boys become aware of this when they become physically aroused by the slightest perception or thought association to their own sexuality. Even fewer know that since the advent of technology and prenatal screening, we know that males experience erection in utero. Presumably females experience comparable sensations but, of course, it would not be visible.

I conclude that we humans are very sexual beings, not merely beings who reproduce sexually, and that we are sexual every moment of our lives. This does not mean that we are acting out genital or even sex-focused sexuality. To me it means that our lives are infused with sexuality. I equate this with vitality, interest, and enthusiasm for life.

my "erotic" to T.K. ?

Furthermore, we are spiritual beings, not just when we are paying attention to the spiritual, but again, every moment of our lives. This can be known but not proven. If it is so, and this I believe with a sense of knowing, then we are inseparably spiritual and sexual. Yet altogether too often, the sexual and spiritual are perceived as being in opposition to each other within our historical culture.

The attitude or belief that our sexual nature and our spiritual nature are in opposition constitutes sexual and psychic wounding since it leads us to feel separation and alienation from our innate nature. Sexual wounding limits our perceptions of ourselves and others. All of us have grown up hearing negative messages about sex and about bodies. Sexuality is further trivialized by the sensational overexposure of comedians and advertising—all of which use the power of sex but add the "socially appropriate" implication that sex is risqué. Its no wonder we become fragmented and confused or defensive about our sexual thoughts, feelings, and actions. My premise is that the natural integration of sexuality and spirituality has been ruptured by culture and the socializing experience.

My work is to create conditions that facilitate sexual healing, thereby allowing clients to enhance their lives and relationships.

If I accept a married man as a client, it's because I've deduced from our conversation that there is a good chance the marriage will benefit as a result of the client's work with me. (What I say about married clients applies also to those in an important relationship.) I ask what they have done and are doing to deepen and enrich the marriage. Are they being honest with their partner about their dissatisfaction? Sometimes the answer is yes, and they have reached a point of frustration. Sometimes their frustration seems justified to me, other times not. My response will depend on my judgment of that. Either way I will be supportive of the client and guide him to persist instead of abandoning his attempt to enjoy a good sex life with his partner.

One day a married man called, and in the course of the conversation, told me his wife was going through a difficult period and he needed some TLC (tender, loving care). Because he was forthcoming in talking about his marriage, I agreed to see him. He said he would call me back.

I was pleasantly surprised a few days later when Jorge called and said, "After talking with you the other day, I sense there is a greater possibility here than my just taking care of my need for TLC. I'd like to share with you what is going on in my situation and discuss how we might proceed. Initially could we do only a verbal session?"

Thus began a rewarding relationship. Jorge's wife was a counselor herself and therefore putting out a lot of energy to others. She was, as well, working on her own issues and had recently become aware that she needed to work through her teenage experience of being molested by her minister. As she did this, she became very uninterested in being sexual with her husband. Since life is never as neat and orderly as we might wish it, there were other family crises happening as well. Jorge was understanding but also feeling pretty desperate. He was feeling deprived and running out of patience. He was also confused about some of the differences in his preferences in rearing his son versus his wife's choices. This particularly interested me as I have experience as a parent and training in parent education. The role of parenting is not given sufficient attention regarding its intrusion into the marital relationship. I suggested we do sessions combining a half hour of talking followed by a massage. We agreed.

Partway through the first massage, Jorge asked if I would be willing to lie beside him on the massage table. He wanted to hold me, if I didn't mind. I'm careful to remain "the director" during an appointment. I won't trade places nor will I usually join a client on the table. Jorge's request did not feel manipulative; I sensed no covert plans to grope me. It felt appropriate, so I agreed.

"May I touch you?"

"Yes."

Jorge stroked me lightly.

"I like your touch."

"Really?"

"Yes, you have a very nice touch. I feel you are sensitive and caring, and I like your touching me."

With a deep sigh, he continued, enjoying the feeling of soft skin under his hands, caressing me gently and nongenitally. He wanted no more massage that day. Before leaving, he told me something that taught me a lot.

"I really needed to be received. That's the most important thing that is missing. Right now my wife doesn't even want to be held. As much as I need to be touched myself now, I really need to feel received. That's a wonderful gift you've given me today."

Jorge wasn't entirely comfortable with seeking sexual sensations with another woman, so we moved slowly. It was particularly easy since he wanted half the massage time to be holding and feeling close. He finally decided that what he was doing was definitely not from selfish motives but realistic need and true desire to preserve and improve his marriage and that it would be okay for him to enjoy climax.

We saw each other about once a month. He and his wife were also in couple counseling, and Jorge was able to weave the processes together. After his wife became pregnant, he thought he wouldn't see me again. Following the birth and the very tiring life following that, however, he came once more to recharge his batteries and say good-bye.

After Jorge put into words the need to be received, I realized how much this applied to so many of my clients. I began discussing this with them and found many men, who hadn't articulated this need to be received, grateful for my understanding. The men who were still having sex with their wives, but finding it too perfunctory, always expressed relief at having their frustration named. They all knew they wanted their wives to desire them; they hadn't realized the extra dimension of their frustration was their need to be wanted and received.

Over time my clients begin to relax and unwind when they are with me. They begin to respond to my sincere interest in them and their lives. They begin to speak of their feelings and especially some of their frustrations. They begin to understand what has been missing for them—not just the physical pleasure of sexual stimulation and release, but the closeness of union. This is not to imply union with me, as ours is a professional and limited relationship. But they do begin to realize their loss of intimacy and its importance to them. Some will respond to my suggestions about opening dialogue with their partner, but most, unfortunately, feel safer sharing intimacy with me. They feel they have been rejected, and they have great need to protect themselves from further sexual rejection.

One of my clients eventually came to share just that with me. Tall, slender, tanned, and silver haired, Lenny began seeing me before I restricted my clientele to those on the spiritual journey. He would listen to my talk of soul and spirituality, holism and healing, and then chuckle indulgently. He smokes, hangs out with buddies in bars, and his exercise is a weekly game of golf. He thinks what I talk about is psychobabble or New Age and doesn't make sense. It might sound good, but it doesn't apply to him or anything he can use. Still, he keeps coming back to see me.

It took him several visits to feel secure and share concerns with me. He reluctantly told me that he lived with his girlfriend "and we don't have sex anymore. She doesn't want to."

"But what about you?"

"I'm here," he said with finality. I took the hint and backed off.

On subsequent visits, I'd be careful not to pry, yet try to learn and understand a little more.

"Thinking about your girlfriend—was sex ever good?"

"At first, yeah."

"You think she enjoyed sex?"

"I thought so then."

"Do you talk together about it?"

"Um, once in a while. She says she just doesn't feel like it."

"Don't you want to revive it?"

"Sure I want a sex life. But I'm not going to beg."

The tone told me it was time to change the conversation. Lenny was not the first client I had heard use the word *beg*. My estimate, based on conversations with many clients, is that a man feels he's begging after being rebuffed on three occasions. Most learn to turn off toward their partner rather than risk further rejection.

Through our conversations I hope to validate my client's sexuality and its importance to him and also help him to understand what might be his partner's reasons for her behavior. If they have just let the sexual slide and it's been some time, I'll suggest courting, reawakening his wife's interest. This especially means that I will press him to be considerate, romantic, to touch and caress his wife and *not* go on to "sex." This is a hard one for most men. But it's probably imperative if the romance has gone. If they have never talked about the lapse of sex in their marriage, I'll strongly urge that they do so and will, in effect, do role-playing with them by suggesting imaginary scenarios.

Most of the time when I steered the conversation in this direction with Lenny he would adroitly steer me away. Finally he told me, "I don't want her taking mercy on me and dutifully obliging."

"I understand—but sex is an important part of life and relationship. You aren't going to let it die, are you?"

"The rest of our relationship is good. We enjoy each other's company and a lot of the same things. I like being together, and it's a long time now."

"How long?"

"Ten years."

"That is a long time. I hope I can persuade you to talk with her and find helpful ways to approach the subject."

"You don't give up easily, do you?"

"I really believe in what I'm doing. All of us deserve to enjoy our sexuality. It's sad how we women frequently let sex go for whatever reasons. I was that way. Ask my first husband! I remarried a man with experience and patience. I thought he wanted altogether too much sex and told him it was all in his head. His body didn't really *need* so much. Without making me wrong, he got me to listen to him and ask myself questions. I certainly became better off for it. Now I *know* how much better I feel when I share sexuality with a partner."

"You know, something odd—I don't mean to be boasting but— the first year we were dating, we had sex every day for a year. I just noticed, I mean, I wasn't counting. But we never missed a day."

"Of course frequency is a lot higher at first but...every day? And now nothing? What happened?"

"We moved in together, and it became less and less frequent."

"Surely you spoke to her?"

"She reminded me that I knew she hadn't had sex with her late husband the last eight years of their marriage and he hadn't complained."

"Are you sure, Lenny, that this is what you want?"

"Everything else is good. I've told you I don't want mercy sex. I enjoy seeing you. I don't know if I come here for the sex or the talk."

I assured Lenny he wasn't unusual. Clients who continue to see me come for the intimacy of sharing honest talk.

Some men still cuddle and touch though their wives don't want sex. In this case, I really support them for taking care of themselves rather than letting their sexuality wither or themselves become bitter. And I want to know how they justify coming to see me. In other words, they have to acknowledge what they are doing and how it might affect their marriage.

I would not be assisting anyone in healing if I were to support them in escapist behavior. Sometimes limiting their sexual expression to the sessions with me is entirely appropriate. They are behaving in a way that is responsible to their relationship. Like Jorge and Lenny, they are not jeopardizing their partners and they are taking care of legitimate needs, giving themselves patience to be loving, caring partners even without sex.

Those who are single may substitute their relationship to me for a personal one. There are a number of reasons they might do this. One is that they are busy with their profession and don't feel they have enough time to give to a love relationship. Another is their shyness, perhaps even a lack of social skills. They may have been emotionally hurt in an earlier relationship and don't want to risk that again. Another reason could be their limited ability to tolerate closeness. In a professional relationship with me they can have brief interludes of closeness, yet the limits preclude any risk of intimacy in the entirety of their lives.

Over time I will guide the conversation to include possibilities of relationship and what might be the reasons for holding back. To single clients, I'll suggest resources, ways to meet others, and help with social skills, if that is needed. Frequently, a man will act as if he thinks the love of his life is going to suddenly appear without any effort on his part—and that he will *know* this is the one. If this is the case, I'll gently tease him about his expectations of this effortless meeting. If it seems appropriate, bit by bit, I'll nudge him to begin efforts for himself.

Thirty-one-year-old Robert was a little shy, a gentle man, good-looking with medium blond hair, a golden complexion, balanced features, and a body kept fit by his participation in sports year-round. From the beginning, Robert loved massage and touch. He quickly became at ease with me and soon was keeping a monthly appointment. Occasionally he would ask me to take a Polaroid photo of him to use in a reply to a personals ad.

He'd tell me about the women he met and the dates they were having. But each relationship seemed to dwindle after a few months. Robert was on a career track in the hotel industry, was a diligent worker with a good future ahead, and yet was definitely not a workaholic. He was also an avid reader. Why did one attempt at relationship after another fail? I was quite puzzled and would tactfully broach the subject.

Robert became more and more easy and relaxed with me. He frequently brought me flowers or some small gift. I became aware he had romantic feelings for me. He finally verbalized his interest. I replied that I was flattered, but he knew I had a relationship and was quite satisfied. At that time, unfortunately, I failed to make it clear that because ours was a professional relationship, it needed to remain so.

Clearly, as time passed, I satisfied emotional needs of Robert. I kept encouraging him to find his own partner, telling him that he had much to offer. I had known him over four years when he finally told me how inexperienced sexually he was. We did verbal sessions about dating and how to approach someone. I asked Robert how he moved from friendship toward greater intimacy.

"Well, you know, you don't want to offend someone by being intrusive."

"True. Maybe the women cool off to you because you remain friendly and don't start expressing romantic interest. Could that be it?"

"Hm…yes."

"Do you hold your date's hand in the movies? Do you kiss her good night?"

Hesitantly, "No…"

"Do you hug?" (This is California, where hugging is pandemic…and I already know what a good hugger Robert is.)

"No."

"No? Why on earth not?"

"Well, you really don't want to offend, you know."

"But humans give signals that show whether they are open or closed to touch, to hugging, to kissing. Do you know how to read those signals?"

"I guess not."

"Well, how about me helping you to learn?"

Robert had no hesitation. I first showed him how to make a neutral touching gesture and notice if the other person stayed relaxed or tightened. If the message was of comfort, then Robert could make a slightly more personal touch. He could let his touch linger. He was nervous about trying, but I convinced him to risk the approach. He reported back that it was getting easier.

Another long time passed when Robert finally told me, on the phone, that he had only experienced sexual intercourse a few times. Could I help him?

At that point we talked about my training as a sexual surrogate. I told him what we might do if he chose to see me for surrogacy sessions. He was to think about it while I did too.

I was no longer in my relationship and was enjoying a period of celibacy. I was learning a lot about my own sexual energy. While I really liked Robert and wanted to help him, not to mention wanting some fortunate woman somewhere to have the pleasure of this man's company, I needed to think through my own situation. I decided that I didn't want to break my celibacy for a work situation, so I didn't push the subject with Robert.

A few months later Robert decided he would like to work this through. I'd already guessed that his earlier experiences had been with women who took the initiative. Robert was still held back by not wanting to offend and make a woman angry.

I explained to Robert that he needed to pick up the signals from his touches and keep going a step further. I told him he must initiate with me and then I would give him strong signals of my interest. Afterward we would go back over our path and I would point out the signals he missed. This was to get to a kiss first, and eventually to touch breasts, to unbutton a blouse, and so on. We were still a long way from intercourse. Finally, Robert was at ease and enjoying caressing and kissing and cunnilingus with me. He was passively following me instead of initiating his own moves.

"Robert, everything you do, you do well. Its clear that I'm enjoying myself. Time for you to take over. From now on, when you come for an appointment, I'll use my usual format and you'll get a wonderful massage—but nothing else unless you initiate. OK?"

"Uh-huh."

The next sessions began with kissing and then to massage. When I refrained from making an opening gesture of embrace, even the kissing stopped. Following each massage, we'd talk and I'd encourage Robert to initiate.

Once when Robert did initiate but did not pursue intercourse and did not go farther with the intimate kissing, I decided I would take us the rest of the way. I was ready to make an exception in my celibate pattern to assist Robert. Robert was shocked and pleased.

He didn't come right away. He would get close and then not be able to let go. There was some powerful inhibition in Robert, and I was concerned that perhaps I needed to refer Robert for counseling to work on deeper issues than shyness. Finally the pleasure washed over and seized control from him....

"Wow!"

"Ummmmm."

"Wow!"

"Uh-huh. *Wow* will do."

Chuckle, and another deep chuckle..."Wow!"

Robert liked this sufficiently to overcome his shyness, and he didn't hesitate to initiate after that.

He started making better contacts with women, sometimes going out with someone from work, other times with a friend of a friend. Robert is forty now and still single. But it's been more than six months since I've seen him. He's seeing someone he's interested in. It's possible that he will have his own rewarding relationship. He'll be a real "catch."

It's not only single or divorced men looking for sex and intimacy who seek out professionals. Married men can be afraid of too much intimacy with their wives.

Lewis sees me infrequently, about every four or five months. He's only mildly sexually frustrated at home, more bored because his wife wants sex in bed in the usual style, "no variations, please."

With me, Lewis shares his frustration about his job, which he no longer finds exciting. He needs to work about another five years to have enough to retire. He also shares his dream of living and traveling on his own boat.

He enjoys being quiet with his own thoughts and likes to putter in the yard or fix problems in his house or work on his car. He's frustrated in this because his wife nags him to hire someone to do the work so that he will be in the house with her. He admits that his wife would probably like to hear his thoughts, but he prefers not to be intimate with her.

"Lewis, you clearly want intimacy or you wouldn't come and share so much of yourself with me. You seem very much at ease with me, even when you talk about your own confusion or short-comings. Why not with your wife?"

"I don't have to live with you."

"What do you mean?"

"What if I say something and then it comes back to haunt me, is used against me? I realize this is my problem and I'm sure my wife would be happy for me to share more. She wants me to stay too close to her though. I need time alone, puttering, to think."

For Lewis, sharing with me has not led to more sharing at home, but he has rewritten his résumé and is discreetly placing it. He doesn't want to rock the boat at home. At least for now, he has also decided not to push for variety and experimentation with his wife.

In addition to helping a client in self-reflection and articulation of feelings, I want for him to integrate his experiences into his ongoing life context. His session with me is not a brief interlude *out* of life but a vital part *of* life. My premise is that the natural integration of sexuality and spirituality has been ruptured by culture and the socializing experience. I want them to see and feel that sexuality is a constant and we don't take time out to "do" or "have" sex. When our minds, bodies, and spirits are whole, we take time to eat, sleep, exercise, socialize, engage in spiritual practice, and nurture our sexuality.

A healthy sexuality does not equate with "genitality." It's *more* than "genitality" and may not even include genital activity. A walk in a meadow, enjoying the sunshine, the flowers, a warm breeze, the movement of our muscles, the encounter of our feet with earth, the quieting of the mind—this too is sexuality, sometimes thought of as sensuality. Some may call this a spiritual experience. I wouldn't quarrel with that. My point of view is that it is simultaneously sexual and spiritual—because every minute of our lives is both.

I see healing needed if we are to live fully and enjoy both our spiritual selves and our sexual selves. Religion and society have created the dichotomy. There is no reason at all to be so dualistic about it. Because our very language is dualistic, it becomes altogether too easy for the mind/body to be perceived as separate without even considering the spiritual dimension. Holistic health means balance and harmony of body and mind and spirit.

As a child, I certainly never dreamed of this work I am doing. From the time I was small, I liked to help people feel good about themselves. In my teens I felt quite drawn toward missionary work…and I was also coming awake sexually and liked kissing and petting. Of course I struggled with the shoulds and shouldn'ts—this was in the '50s. Sex won out over spirituality at that time. I married and had my first child at eighteen. By the time my second child was born when I was twenty, I was seriously questioning my religion. The woman I wanted for godmother to my daughter did not believe in original sin. Neither did I, but the Episcopal priest did and explained that baptism was for remission of that sin. I had thought baptism was welcoming a newcomer into the family of worshippers.

By my mid-twenties I had become a humanist and followed this by getting a bachelor's degree in humanistic psychology. I wasn't consciously aware of my spiritual life and didn't feel anything missing. In my mid-thirties I was surprised to find myself living in a spiritual commune with folk who believed in God. I was willing to study the book these people were reading and went to the library frequently to refute what the book was asserting. To my astonishment, I found that many great thinkers throughout history had been believers. I had not previously thought religion to be a thinking person's game.

Slowly I was changed. I finally knew God, not as a terrifying judge but as a loving parent. For several years I both prayed to know God's will for me and wondered how one could know that. Just deciding that what I think is God's will would not do because there were too many examples in history of terror and tragedy in the name of God.

I finally decided that when one is doing what one is on this planet to do, the doors open. When the doors close, it's time to recognize I am on the wrong path.

My next step, growing out of my reflection on my past, was the serendipitous encounter with an announcement inviting volunteers to study human sexuality in a training program to become telephone volunteers on an answering line. I *knew* this was it.

The semester-long training class included much self–examination and verbal exchange with fellow trainees, preparing us to help the callers to the information line. When I finally was volunteering weekly, I found great satisfaction. The line's purpose was to provide accurate sexual information in a sex-positive manner. This meant condoning only activity that was consensual. I made no changes in my own sexual behavior during that year, but I listened to others' reports of their explorations. Finally I took an introductory workshop that included touch but no overt sex.

I began dating—and playing. This was before AIDS and I knew, and so did the people I played with, how to be responsible regarding sexually transmitted diseases—using protection and making prophylactic visits to the VD clinic every few months. This exploration into my sexuality revealed more to me about myself than I expected. I enjoyed this period of time. I was living alone for the first time and dating a variety of men. I used to joke that I was forty-two going on sixteen.

I was also pursuing a master's degree in a seminary and exploring another career direction. The field of sex therapy is where I was feeling drawn.

I did some volunteer projects, including one on sex education in a junior high school. After training as a sex surrogate, I spent several months reflecting on the future. It became clear that I didn't want to focus on specific physical sexual problems, as is often the case for sex surrogates, but preferred to help people work through their contradictory sex attitudes as I had done before the surrogate training.

I had experienced many bodywork therapies to relieve my ongoing back pain. Interested in the body–mind connection, eventually I added massage therapy to my training. And so over a period of five years I changed from being a kindergarten teacher to a woman with my own massage practice combining much of my background and interests.

My work has evolved and so have I. When I began, I was not very at ease with men. And truth to tell, I wasn't very trusting or favorably disposed toward them either. But I felt strongly drawn to my work. As I came to know so many men from so many different backgrounds and walks of life, I came to appreciate the humanness of men. I came to see how emotionally and spiritually hungry many men are and how much they are looking for kindness and understanding.

I feel privileged to have been guided into the work I do. I'm both broadened and deepened by my work in sexuality and massage. This work has also supported my worldly needs and has added to my personal sense of confidence. Spiritually, I was guided to a church that emphasizes personal prayer and meditation. I became a lay minister in that church and received the confidence of the minister in my work, such that she referred couples to me.

I feel graced by my work, my friends, and my clients. People who know me are accepting of my work, even when it raises questions for them. More recently, on a one-to-one basis, when I speak with other health professionals about my work in sexuality, massage, and spirituality, I find understanding and approval.

My next step, I feel, is to share with a larger public what I have learned.

CAROL QUEEN

❦

THE CALL GIRL

Introduction to

CAROL QUEEN

The chant went something like this:

> Listen, listen, listen to my heart's song.
> Listen, listen, listen to my heart's song.
> I will never forget you, I will never forsake you.
> I will never forget you, I will never forsake you.
>
> Listen, listen, listen to my heart's song.
> Listen, listen, listen to my heart's song.
> I will always be with you, I will always remember.
> I will always be with you, I will always remember.

Our friends, lovers, and family members had died or were dying from AIDS, and these were the words Carol Queen was leading us in as we sang swaying side to side, holding hands in a

circle. This hymn adapted from the ancient Old Religion was a fit-
ting benediction to complete a cross-dressing role-playing session.
Some of us were men dressed as women, some women as men, some
were nude, some in leather, some in feathers. It was a weeklong
safe-sex intensive training for sex therapists, nurses, AIDS counselors, and other professionals dedicated to sex-positive AIDS
education.

When I first met Carol, she had completed a year of graduate
school in sociology and had just switched to the field of sexology.
She was obviously bright and very articulate. Moreover, she was
willing to be forthright; she finds it empowering to be publicly out
of the closet about the whole of her sexual life—from heterosexual
to lesbian to bisexual, from a passionate love relationship with her
former high school teacher twice her senior, to her life in "The Life"
of whoredom, as she calls it.

Carol once described herself as a nerd turned call girl. When
she walked around naked wearing nothing but her black-framed
glasses on the set for an orgasm documentary in which we both
were being interviewed, she truly fit her self-applied label. Carol,
however, is far more than a free spirit, sexually active intellectual.
Through her increasing number of public speaking engagements
around the country and her numerous essays and erotica writings,
she is becoming a popular spokesperson for sexuality outside the
mainstream.

In a first impression, one might think Carol is sweet and perky,
a little bit of a modern-day, punkish Debbie Reynolds (the slightly
sexy, all-American sweetheart in the '50s). Actually, when Carol is
championing not-so-politically-correct sexual views, language, and
lifestyles (such as in her recent book, *Exhibitionism for the Shy*), she
almost makes Bad Girl Madonna look like a Good Girl.

Yet, in all of Carol's outrageousness, I have never heard bitterness or resentment from her though there have been many

narrow-minded reactions to her choices that have made her a sexual, political, and religious outlaw. Were this only a couple of centuries ago, she would have been burned at the stake for her beliefs and behaviors as a queer, a whore, and a witch.

Carol is a follower of the Old Religion, which worships the Goddess as well as male deities. Many of the adherents refer to the loose network of closely knit groups as the Wiccan tradition. Before the Christian Church of Rome and later some Protestants for over almost five centuries carried forth their ethnic cleansing atrocities, murdering and burning at the stake perhaps up to nine million so-called witches (both female and male), many Earth-centered, Goddess-oriented religions flourished throughout Europe and the Middle East. Now many of the Wiccan followers meet in secrecy, most never revealing publicly their spiritual truths or identity. Here too Carol is out of the closet, as she writes in the following chapter: "After seven thousand years of oppression, I declare this the time to bring back our temple."

She genuinely feels she is doing the Goddess's sacred work in the world. She believes that prostitutes, whether they see themselves as "sacred" prostitutes or as "secular" prostitutes, can and do make a major contribution to humanity.

Carol is definitely making a contribution. Her actions and her words are a voice singing the sacred song of the often maligned, often overly romanticized world's oldest profession: listen, listen, listen to my heart's song.

THE CALL GIRL

by

Carol Queen

Christianity gave Eros poison to drink; he did not die of it, but degenerated into a vice.

Nietzsche

My lover just bought a sex encyclopedia published in 1935, the kind of volume that begins with a scholarly introduction and then proceeds to define all sorts of sex-related words and phrases. Among the definitions, some archaic and amusing and some quite up-to-date, we found some interesting things. Under *Prostitution*, the author wrote: "The history of prostitution is an exceedingly long and checkered one, reaching back, in fact, beyond history itself, its origin being lost in dimmest antiquity. It is not by any means, as moralists sometimes imply, a phenomenon peculiar to our own degenerate times; rather it is likely of lesser extent to-day than in former times. We find it referred to in the Old Testament as an extremely widespread and very ancient institution" (Adolph F. Niemoeller, *American Encyclopedia of Sex*, p. 215).

This entry was followed by another: "*Prostitution, sacred, religious, or temple.* A form of prostitution important in pagan antiquity in which sexual pleasures and intercourse formed part of the cult of certain gods and goddesses whose worship entailed sensual gratification, the surrender of bodily chastity, and the like. This could take many different forms: the priestesses of the temple could be prostitutes and always available for ardent worshipers, the fees from the commerce going into the temple's coffers; or the creed could require (as Herodotus tells of the Babylonian law) that each woman go once in her lifetime to sit before the temple…and there remain until some stranger chose her for coition, first throwing silver on her knees…" (Niemoeller, p. 216).

My "ardent worshipers" and I have no temple today in which to perform a dance that sometimes seems more profane than sacred. In a culture that does not worship the Goddess, these are degenerate times indeed, but not because a once-holy act is still being negotiated in hotel suites, in massage parlors, on city streets. In fact, if prostitution is ever eradicated, it will be a signal that Christianity's murder of Eros is complete, the Goddess's rule completely overturned. Perhaps most prostitutes today are unaware that their profession has a sacred history, and doubtless most clients would define what they do with us as something other than worship. But I believe that an echo of the old relationship, when he was seeker and she was Source, are still present when money changes hands today.

I tell my own story to explore the ancient resonance within modern prostitution, and to encourage others to consider the profession in a way that departs from the stereotypes fed us by Hollywood movies, morals crusaders, and *Miami Vice*.

❦

I was called to the oldest calling five years ago, and it was quite unexpected. I did not seek prostitution out, although I can remember fantasizing about being a prostitute when I was a very young girl. Some of my earliest sexual reveries involved being paid to do sexual things with a shadowy stranger of a man. But by the time my adult sexual persona was taking shape, late in adolescence, I had put those fantasies away. Influenced by feminism, I would probably have said that women should have the right to do what they wished with their bodies but that selling them was degrading.

It is a source of great wonder to me, having lived the knowledge (or perhaps I should say *a knowledge*) of prostitution in my body, that the intellectual resources of feminism, its powerful theory, should shore up conservative Christianity's position on this question. The two worldviews have in common a reluctance to listen to the voices of women who do *not* experience sexwork as degrading. I began to believe when I was quite young that Christianity was no friend to an emerging, adventurous sexuality. Later I read some history which backed up my intuitive judgment. (There are millennia-old reasons for Christianity's sex antipathy; I'll explore some below.)

My feminist-influenced beliefs about prostitution were shaken when, as part of my graduate study in sexology, I began to meet perfectly intelligent women who had much more complex things to say about their lives as prostitutes than I would have expected. It was only this that prepared me for an offer from a new friend when I was in transition, at the end of a relationship.

"You've got to get your own apartment!" she said. (I was staying with friends while I pondered my next step.)

"I can't afford one yet," I told her. I'd been going to school and my savings were low.

"That's ridiculous! You can afford anything you want! Money's not hard to get. You should do what *I* do!"

I was truly puzzled. I thought she was a counselor. That's what it said on her card.

"No, silly! I'm a prostitute!"

Like the mature and well-spoken women who'd discussed their lives as call girls in front of a college class, my friend Sally was not your typical whore. I had no idea she spent her days having sex for money in the sunny apartment where we were having coffee and this conversation. At that point, I also had no idea that the "typical whore"—that imaginary creature—does not exist.

Sally disabused me of some of my notions about what it must be like to make a living having sex with strangers. It could be quite a living, for one thing; $150 to $200 a session was the going rate for women in her circle. I would not have to do anything I didn't want to do with a client; I would be in full control, including setting my own standards of safe-sex. If a client and I got along, he would likely call me over and over—making even my idea that prostitution involved having sex with "strangers" only partly true. Most women she knew, Sally said, relied on these "regulars" for both financial comfort and a sense of continuity. And she laughed at my questions about the men who dropped such large sums for an hour or so of company—why did they need to visit whores?

"You won't *believe* some of the men," she said.

I decided to take Sally up on her offer to introduce me to a couple of madams she knew and worked with. If they liked me, I could get referrals from them, and they would start me out with clients they knew well, so they could tell me what to expect with each one. True, I knew I could use the money. But more than that, I was intrigued. What better way to learn about prostitution than to try it? I resolved that I would continue only if my first few forays felt comfortable, and that I would only agree to see a client if I could feel connected to him in some way, through arousal or a sense of fellowship.

I spoke to friends about my decision. My sexual journey had already led me to spend a decade in the lesbian and gay community, and I applied its politics of "coming out," disclosing my apart-from-the-norm sexual identity as instinctively with prostitution as I did as a lesbian or a bisexual. How else, if people don't come out, can a person with no experience of a particular sexuality—especially given the raging proliferation of stereotypes—come to understand why others prefer or behave differently? (It is in this spirit, too, that I write this essay—because I have a store of information and a perspective that many others do not, and because, unlike many whores, I do not live my life in secret.)

Some of my friends were shocked and upset. Some gave me support, however hesitant. I found I could not predict how a friend would react to the news. One woman has not spoken to me since. One, a phone-fantasy worker herself, went into a lather because I would be having actual contact with my clients—to her, talk was fine, but touch was unacceptable. One friend, a lesbian who'd never had enjoyable sex with a man, was unconditional in her respect for my decision. The most important disclosure—to my brand-new lover—led to a conversation in which he revealed that *he* had had sex for money a few times when he was younger.

My two madams could not have been more different. One, Antoinette, was a mature woman with a family to support. The other, Angelica, was younger than I and, aside from running a tight business ship, was a party girl who seemed to have every well-to-do man in the Bay Area in her Rolodex. The only thing the two seemed to have in common, in fact, were their bulging phone books. Each took a commission of 25 to 35 percent when she made a match between client and prostitute. Both of them also still saw clients themselves.

Another quality I saw they shared after I had been working with them for some time was this: Unlike some of the women who worked for them, neither ever expressed contempt for their clients or any sort of revulsion about the men's sexual desires. This surely contributed to their success as madams, but more than that, I see it as one trait of the sexual priestess who accepts all who come to her. These women oversee what is left of the temples, the ruins that are our legacy from a time when desire could be venerated by religion. Some of our folk heroes in America are madams—I am thinking especially of Sally Stanford, the Sausalito madam turned mayor, and some of the women of the Wild West, who could wield great influence at a time and a place when morality depended on a different set of criteria than were enforced back East. Perhaps madams, with what seems like unconditional acceptance, represent a sort of sexualized motherly love. I find it ironic, given the way madams hearken back to the times of the erotic priestesses, that they are prosecuted much more harshly than ordinary prostitutes when they are caught. In California the prostitute's first arrest is on a misdemeanor charge, but the madam faces a felony conviction. Perhaps this is the legacy of Judeo-Christian law with its emphasis on bringing down those who possess Goddess-given power. It also serves to prevent the temples of priestesses from forming again.

Antoinette sent me my first client. He was an older man, she said, who lived alone. His sexual response was very dependent on fantasy. I would have to be talkative.

A wealthy, urbane grandfather answered the door when I rang the bell. I was nervous as a cat, but he assured me that I must know much more about sex than he did—I was studying it, after all, and he had just stumbled through, his whole life. He had been a widower for years. But his wife was more present to him as we went to his bedroom than the very much alive spouses of almost every subsequent client I have had: he wanted to talk about her as we had sex.

He told me not to bother touching his cock; he hadn't gotten an erection in years. "I'm just too old for that," he said. "I'm as limp as that flag out there," and he gestured to a banner hanging outside, still in the windless night air. But he masturbated vigorously, working his soft cock so rapidly his hand was a blur, and I held him while he did, and we made up a story.

"My wife—you would have loved her. She was a luscious woman. All curves. Her tits were this big." He held his hands out, cantaloupe-sized breasts with his palms curved around them. "You like that, don't you? She loved sex. We used to do it every day. If you saw her in the market you would definitely notice her. What would you do, if you saw a woman like that?"

"Oh, yes," I tried to catch the wave of his thoughts, "she's too beautiful not to notice! I love women who are older than me. I'd round the corner in the market near my house and see her—it would make me catch my breath! But I don't know how to approach strangers in public. I would hope that she noticed me too. I would look over my shoulder every few minutes to see if she was still near me. I would try to discover something about her by looking at the things she bought."

"She is only there to look for someone like you. She had a powerful appetite, my wife. She has noticed you and is following you around the market. She is very bold, not shy like you are. She will probably follow you home."

"I'm not expecting anyone—when the doorbell rings, it startles me! I look through the peephole, and there she is, that beautiful woman from the market! My heart is pounding when I let her in. What does she want?"

"She wants you! She wants to make love to you! Ohhhhh…"

The old man was so close to orgasm. He could not possibly need me to have this fantasy—he probably put himself to sleep with it every night. My role must be to witness this desire that lived years after the desired one died, and to confirm it, to add a note of unpredictability to his fantasy.

"She doesn't say a word to me—she just reaches out and pulls me to her! She begins to kiss me and my head is spinning. She takes my hands and puts them on her breasts—I know she must mean she wants me to squeeze them. My god, they're so big and luscious…"

"Ohhhhh…"

"I don't know what's happening to me! It's like I'm possessed! I am scrambling to get my hands under her shirt—I have to touch those breasts! God, they're so full and soft…I have to do this, I can't help myself…she has such a powerful effect on me…I am sucking her nipples now, oh, they're so big and sweet, I have to suck your wife's lovely breast…"

"Ohh…oh…oh…ohhhhh!" His body, still in my arms, shook as he came. But as soon as his orgasm was over, he scurried in to the bathroom to wash the ejaculate off his hands. I lay in his big bed, looking at the pictures of his grandchildren on the bureau and thinking that nothing I thought I knew about men's sexuality had prepared me for the experience I'd just had.

He came out wrapped in a big white robe that, as it turned out, had two hundred-dollar bills tucked into the pocket. He slipped these to me as he kissed my cheek and warned me to be safe getting home. "You're a sweet girl," he said.

❦

Working with sex in a field in which most of my clients are men has meant to me above all that I could challenge my own stereotypes about male sexuality. The old widower was not the only client whose eroticism depended upon the realm of fantasy, nor was he the only client I've had who did not touch my pussy. I thought that as a prostitute I would professionally suck and fuck, but I have also cross-dressed clients, masturbated in front of them so they could watch me ejaculate in a musky little rainstorm, played with their nipples and assholes, and dabbled in watersports[1] and dominance and submission. I have also had clients who insisted upon thinking of me as their lover, whose connection with sex was incomplete without a "real" relationship—even if it, too, was fantasy.

I was deeply affected by that first client, and in fact I felt very privileged to be with someone who had discovered a way to so uniquely mold sexual energy to his needs. Of course, not every subsequent client had this capacity. Many saw sex the way I'd thought most men did—a little sucking, a little fucking, a little breast fondling along the way, and they seemed perfectly satisfied that they had gotten their money's worth. I don't mean to imply that there is anything wrong with meat-and-potatoes sex—I had a great time with many of these clients—but I especially liked working with the ones whose sexual interests were more complicated. These were the men whom many other prostitutes didn't understand, and sometimes found unacceptably "kinky."

I came to believe that the men who were my clients—mostly "yuppies and their dads," as I usually describe them—were paying for sex *not* because they couldn't get it any other way, as I had assumed before I met them. After all, most of them, I'd guess 90 percent or more, were married or partnered. Rather, the men, mostly successful businessmen, paid for sex because it was more

---

[1] *Watersports* refers to erotic play involving urine.

convenient to do so than to find partners any other way, and because extracurricular sex with prostitutes didn't carry as much risk to their marriages as taking a mistress might. I also had the feeling that most of the "kinky" clients had a different kind of sex with me than they had at home. While the other guys were basically looking for erotic variety, the fetishistic men were coming to me to get sexual needs met that were secret, saved for these forays into the sexual underworld that took the pressure off, that let them go back home without having to try to involve their wives in sexual negotiations for preferences the husbands were hesitant to admit.

I knew about the history of the sacred priestess/whores before I began whoring, and I came to feel a very real resonance with this archetype as I collected more diverse experiences with clients. In antiquity the temple whores let worshippers experience, on a body level, the compassionate, passionate Goddess; was that not what I was doing, albeit in a context without overt spiritual meaning? But it *does* have spiritual meaning to me. I have been involved in Wicca's ritualistic Goddess worship for many years; it is the only Western religion whose deity says, "All acts of love and pleasure are My rituals." Wicca has some of its roots in more ancient Goddess-worshipping religions which made sex a powerful sacrament. The Christians have misnamed these as "fertility cults," gutting their religious significance and altering their real meaning.

When a client comes to me, he brings need of a kind he often cannot articulate. His need for acceptance and nurturance is intermingled with erotic longing. At first I was surprised to open the door to men I had never met before and find that they were already erect, but now I see this as a body understanding on the client's part that his desire will be accepted and affirmed. He does not feel desire for a particular person, but the sort of desire, I am certain, that ardent worshippers brought to the temples, desire to connect, to know eroticism as powerful and good. Today, unless he is a pagan

or a Tantrika, he probably does not have the language to acknowledge his desire to go to the Goddess's arms, but something archetypal is happening in him nonetheless.

And something archetypal is certainly happening to me as I
invite him in. I work in my home; it and my body are my temples.
The act of prostitution, no matter which specific sexual act I perform, has a ritualism about it: I dress, choosing clothes that convey a
sense of eroticism; I bathe when the man has gone, the money he
leaves behind proof that our relationship, and our relations, are of a
specialized kind. I know he will not stay for dinner, and he is not
my lover, though love—and not just physical love—passes between
me and my clients very routinely. If he is a stranger, I treat him as if
we have known each other always. The ways in which our interac-
tions are circumscribed—even by our use of condoms and other
forms of safe-sex—give them a particular intensity.

I need not have worried about whether I would feel arousal or
fellowship with my clients. I have never turned a man away, though
I am sure I would if my intuition told me it was best. "Money is the
best aphrodisiac!" some whores profess, and there is something to
that, but for me the sexual energy comes as if unbidden because I
am in sexual *and* spiritual space.

I don't mean to make prostitution, even done with spiritual
meaning, sound effortless. We are doing the Goddess's work in a
culture that would still like to label it the Devil's, after all. It is not
legal; it is stigmatized. I had almost grown brave enough to write
my mother a letter telling her about my life in The Life (as the street
whores call it) when she died, making the conversation unnecessary but the absence of it particularly resonant. Sex was a nemesis in
her life—probably the way it is for many of my clients' wives. She
had never found a way to make it enjoyable, much less sacred.
Everything in her life—except, I guess, my father—supported her
in this antipathy. I will always wonder whether anything about my

so very different path might have illuminated her experience in a new way. And I wonder too if our relationship would have survived her probable horror at my choices.

Many of my clients have been scarred by a pervasive negative view, so influenced by an unfriendly, conservative Christianity, of sex and pleasure. Not every client comes to me joyful or even leaves joyful. In fact, with many men, I see the curtain descend right after orgasm, and their open emotions close, their countenances go blank. Some are bitter about women, about sex. Their schizophrenic upbringing as men, after all, taught them that sex was wrong *and* that they should be able to have all of it they wanted. They are engaged in a hurtful dance with women that is powered by resentment and prolonged by their (and their women's) inability to communicate successfully about the forbidden and the intimate. I feel this hurt and this bitterness and can do nothing but aim above it; only sometimes do I feel that I succeed. Other men are sure that their behavior is wrong, and it takes all of the Goddess's love—and all my energy—to provide a safe place for unsullied desire to emerge.

I know in my soul that it is cultural handicaps like these, worn like wounds, that lead some men to violence against prostitutes. I have lived The Life safely for many reasons: I do not live in my body like a victim, I am educated and not lower class, and my clients come to me through someone else's referral, so they have been screened. But I recognize sometimes the frustration about sex and desire that would under other circumstances burst out fiercely.

At the other end of the continuum are the clients who accept themselves, and they are a pleasure to work with because with them I can truly access the feeling that I am doing sacred work. Antoinette called me another time to see a man with a fetish for pubescent girls. "Dress young," she said, "very young." So I put on Mary Janes and a cotton undershirt instead of a bra, tied my hair in a ponytail, and went off to see what sort of adventure this would be.

I was an innocent ten year old, to be seduced, of course, by an older man. He was a gentle fellow in his fifties, and something about the connection I had with him enabled me to stay in my little-girl character until I had thoroughly lost my innocence. After orgasm, when the power of fantasy fades, I asked him to tell me more about his fetish.

"Oh, I have always desired young girls," he said. "For many years I was sexually involved with them. But then about twenty years ago I read an article that indicated that the little girls might not experience this in a healthy way, that it might upset them and affect their adjustment when they got older. I had never considered that my fun with the girls could have such an effect. So I stopped. Later I discreetly offered money to as many of them as I could find, for therapy, if they needed it. I never wanted to hurt them in any way. I loved them.

"So now I live out this preference with women like you."

This is exactly the strategy that a progressive sex therapist would recommend for a man with his "problem," though of course if he lived in another culture his preferences might be accepted and even honored by all, including the young girls he desires. He had devised a way to keep his sexual focus intact against social odds. My wide, "innocent" eyes as he showed me his cock allowed me to dance with him on a tightrope of opprobrium, helped ensure that he stayed healthy in his sexuality, *and* kept little girls emotionally safe.

So many sexual possibilities are not taught or acknowledged in this culture. Miraculously, some people's forbidden desires grow and flower despite all attempts to stunt them. The wisdom of the sadomasochism community—that virtually anything can be done consensually and with a high degree of safety—is silenced, except in that community's own little enclaves. We use sex and desire to sell everything from odorless armpits to cars, yet treating sex as a service commodity is forbidden, the service providers branded as criminals. In fact, we barely treat sex as something to learn about, a set of skills, a knowledge base. Attempts made to educate people, especially young ones, about birth control and safe-sex are attacked.

There was a time when the priestesses in the temple performed sexual initiations and sexual instruction. In the Tantric temples of India, worshippers came to circle the priestess and priest, embodiments of Shakti and Shiva, as they fucked—and this was holy! Children brought to the temple to observe this understood as they grew that sex could take them to a place of loss-of-self, unity-with-all, Enlightenment.

Anthropology teaches us that each culture has its taboos, and often if we study the social structures of a culture we understand why its taboos developed. The temples in which the Goddess was revered came under attack because the religion they represented was under siege: the Bible means it very literally when it blasts "the Whore of Babylon," but it does not teach that she was a *sacred* whore, a priestess. Preceding earliest Judeo-Christian history, the Goddess reigned for aeons. In her book *When God Was a Woman*, Merlin Stone deconstructs the Bible's cautionary tale of Adam and Eve and argues that every symbol in that chapter, from the Tree of Knowledge to the serpent to the apple, was sacred to the Goddess: Genesis is actually an allegory of the struggle between competing religious faiths.

Is it any wonder, then, that the powerful sacred rite done in the Goddess's name, and by extension sexuality itself, was deemed by many early Christians dangerous? And is it any wonder that the history of Western culture since then has included in all epochs a war between Christianity and paganism, hedonism, sexual deviation? The old temples' sacred practices, including prostitution, transvestism, and sodomy (for males sometimes cross-dressed and took the role of priestesses, and men also offered themselves up in

the name of the Goddess), have become the new order's most hei-
nous sexual sins.

Kvos —> true

[Eros did not die of poisoning, and will not—the most life
affirming of all human drives cannot die.[But every child made to
feel ashamed of her own impulses, every adult whose sexual practices are still criminalized, every couple who can't talk about sex
and desire, everyone who is given the green light to hate those who
are sexually different from themselves, has been poisoned. They are
all the victims of that ancient religious war, which in the sexual arena
has never reached a state of truce.

❦

Most prostitutes today would tell you that they do it for the
money, but that is only part of the story. Many women would never
perform sex for money, impoverished or not. What differentiates
the ones who do? Perhaps, as the Religious Right and some feminists proclaim, many women are prostitutes against their will; but
why focus on them without giving equal attention to those women
(and men, for men share the profession at all levels) who *elect* to do
sex as work? What do they have to teach? What will they say that
we are not supposed to hear?

Many will state that they feel good about their profession; they
enjoy providing others satisfaction; they like feeling in control of
their own work situation; they like the sex and the adventure; they
consider prostitution healing.

They are the heirs, whether aware of it or not, of the sacred
priestesses who opened their robes to strangers and revealed the
glowing body of the Goddess.

The Goddess movement today is a vital subculture, exploring

compassionate, feminist/humanist values that go against the grain of our contemporary culture of glorified death. Yet most of the attention given to the newly revived Goddess portrays her in maternal terms: Earth Mother, Mother Goddess. Only a few Goddess scholars emphasize the powerful role that sexuality played in the ancient Goddess's worship. One of Inanna's names was "She of the Wondrous Vulva." Our culture has been made sensitive by Freud to the place where maternal love and sexual love converge, and the Goddess movement's challenge today is to reconcile the age-old, Judeo-Christian dichotomy of the mother and the whore. Perhaps only actual whores know how closely linked the needs for these kinds of love can be.

One client came to me with an attitude that reminded me of a cocky, greedy little boy's. (Certainly one persona I recognize in many clients is that little boy who says, "Gimme!") As he was dressing to leave he began a ramble that seemed bizarre to me at the time but makes sense in retrospect: "Hey, you know, you oughta have kids. You'd make a really good mother. I mean it. How can you not want to have children of your own?"

Another client, whose sexual persona was very submissive, would whimper, "Mommy! Mommy!" just before he came.

Every whore has seen this aspect of desire: the need for Mommy, for maternal caring, for unconditional love. Few adults have anything that feels like this in their lives; we are not even, as mature grown-ups, supposed to want it. Love is sexualized in this culture partly, I think, because sex *does* lead into a sea of love, if we are fortunate enough to be open to it, but also because sex is the one arena in which most adults get touched, stroked, held—all the things it hurt so much to give up as growing kids. Sex reminds us of love even when we have no love in our lives.

❦

I believe that sex is sacred and healing. This idea pervades my work as a prostitute, and this vantage point often startles people accustomed to negative ideas about sexworkers' lives. They press me to delve into the negative side, and it often seems that what they're really looking for is evidence that men who patronize prostitutes are contemptible. I don't believe this; I believe that every client, every *person*, has the right to seek out sexual pleasure and comfort. I've been treated with a good deal more respect by 99 percent of my clients than by the average guy on the street.

Besides prostitution's stigmatized status and the way our sex-negative society makes it hard for both prostitutes and their clients to be proud of themselves, however, I *do* believe there is something wrong with the picture. The problem isn't with prostitution, though, but with sexist social norms. Virtually all of the clients are men, whether the prostitutes they patronize are male or female. The options for women who might like to arrange to see a prostitute are far slimmer.

Surely there are many women who would (at least if social standards were different) appreciate the touch of a sexual healer, the chance to have a great fuck without the entanglements of a relationship, the option to try sexual things they've fantasized about, erotic comfort when lonely, and the embrace of the Goddess. These are all among the reasons men seek out sex professionals. Like men, some women would seek out male sexworkers for access to these experiences and some would choose females.

Any situation that is stereotyped by gender immediately arouses my suspicion. Men are expected to be more sexual than women, so the assertively sexual woman, whether she is seeking her own sexual pleasure or using her body and her sexual prowess for her livelihood, faces acute social disapproval. This is one of the hurdles a woman in this culture must leap to become a sex professional, and a chief source of the stigma she faces: as a woman, she is not supposed to be highly sexual in the first place. Not only has she stepped across the line of social acceptance to become a whore, she has thereby proved herself a slut. Yet many women are highly sexual—some of these gravitate to prostitution as a profession, but others must create a strategy that lets them be both sexual and safe from the acute social disapproval that is the whore's lot. When women's sexual choices are restricted to madonna and whore, good girl and bad girl, many women are forced to walk a narrow path to find "acceptable" outlets for sexual desire and adventure. Still others are frustrated, locked between their appetites and limited social/sexual options.

I am sure there is a class of women in this country wealthy and powerful enough to call upon sexworkers for erotic attention. But for the rest of us, in spite of the gains made by the women's movement, calling a prostitute rarely seems like an option. Almost without exception, the only women I know who have patronized prostitutes have been sexworkers themselves.

I was once called to see a married couple who lived in a wealthy suburb. It was clear from the start that the woman was as much a participant as the man, and at first I thought that I had been called so that she could have a bisexual experience. She seemed completely at ease and passionate. Only when we had been playing for some time did she talk about experiences she had had, years before, as a prostitute.

Male culture allows for the existence of prostitution even when it does not honor it. Having sex with a prostitute is a possibility for virtually any man. Female culture allows the possibility of *becoming* a prostitute, although this is an option "polite society" forbids; but nowhere do we hear acknowledgment that access to sexual service might improve some women's lives. As one result, women's sexual possibilities are more closely involved with their relationships than many men's; for the woman with no relationship or one that is sexually stunted, options are severely narrowed.

❦

To guide another person to orgasm, to hold and caress, to provide companionship and initiation to new forms of sex, to embody the Divine and embrace the seeker—these are healing and holy acts. Every prostitute can do these things, whether or not s/he understands their spiritual potential. For us to see ourselves as sacred whores, for our clients to acknowledge the many facets of desire they bring to us, can be a powerful shift in consciousness. We show the face of the Goddess in a culture that has tried for millennia to break and denigrate Her, just as some today claim *we* are broken and denigrated. They are not correct, and the Goddess will not be broken. In our collective extraordinary experience, we prostitutes have healed even those who do not honor us. Were the attack on us over, we could begin to heal the whole world.

After seven thousand years of oppression, I declare this the time to bring back our temple.

Stephanie Rainbow Lightning Elk

❧

The FireWoman

Introduction to

Stephanie Rainbow Lightning Elk

Stephanie walked up to me saying she had just had an orgasm. Doing nothing sexual, she had simply been lying on a large, flat boulder bridging a stream, connecting deeply with the energies of the boulder.

We had been drawn to this boulder while exploring a canyon in Utah, a canyon that probably had been ceremonial grounds for Native Americans centuries ago. As we continued exploring, we discovered several more "charged" boulders, all basically in a straight line leading across a meadow toward the several-hundred-foot-high waterfall coming off the massive sheer cliff on the western wall of the canyon. Heavy, "energized" stones arranged in a purposeful order have been found in Europe in such places as Stonehenge, but little has been noted about such developments by indigenous peoples of the American Southwest.

Stephanie is quiet, reflective, and very determined. At times she may seem secretive or mysterious to those who are unfamiliar with shamanism: orgasms while communing with a rock is an extremely unlikely topic in any sex-ed class and nothing Masters and Johnson probably ever questioned. Having orgasmic experiences while worshipping "Nature" however is not uncommon for Stephanie—about ten years ago she was drawn to the shamanic path.

Shaman, originally derived from a name used for certain healers in the Ural Mountains of Russia, is now a term applied to women and men worldwide who have developed "extraordinary" abilities to utilize energies of the plant, animal, mineral, human, and spirit worlds. Such people often are members of indigenous cultures and are usually healers and sages, sometimes using "teacher plants," crystals, and intense ceremonies to access powers not comprehended by scientific paradigms.

Since indigenous people have been burned at the stake or have had dogs set upon them because the indigenous spiritual beliefs did not conform to a conquering group's theology, much shamanic knowledge has been lost to the winds of time, especially anything concerning sexual energy. Some teachings have survived by going underground, becoming tightly guarded secrets by rigorously initiated members of shamanic lineages.

Now some of these lineages, concerned about a possible planetary destruction by unwise industrial and political actions, are beginning to re-reveal teachings to the general culture by initiating non-indigenous women and men who then become bicultural messengers—the teachings now following a consciousness line rather than a bloodline. Being profoundly moved by these shamanic teachings, Stephanie Rainbow Lightning Elk (her Medicine name) has committed herself to a new role, one in some ways foreign and in some ways familiar to her European-American upbringing.

Born Martha Stephanie Wadell, Stephanie grew up in the provincial South during the '50s. A description she once wrote about her father suggests why she did not become a typical "Southern belle."

> Being Catholic was unusual in my small southern town in north Florida. Panama City was dominated by the Baptists. They had churches on every block. I knew we were different. We were a minority. My father was always proud of this. His parents had traveled to America from Hungary, seeking the promise of freedom and opportunity. He felt the same and instilled a vision in me: to be different is to be special, set apart, following our own rules. "Why do you want to be like everyone else?" he would ask, his large, sensuous mouth captivating my awareness. "One day you might be president of the United States!" His sky-blue eyes challenged me to think for myself; to be different meant that I could be president of the United States. I was able to fantasize about my future.

Her mother, who was of "strong Celtic descent," had an equally important influence on Stephanie during her youth: "My mother would share with me how powerful her sexual feelings were regarding my father. She described how he would kiss and breathe into her mouth. Other sensual stories from her younger days ignited and inflamed my imagination and innocent sexual stirrings. It was her sharing with me so freely that has gifted me with the freedom to seek and find a profound knowledge of passion. I knew that she was passing on to me with her voice and her body the mysteries of the universe."

Stephanie's Celtic ancestry, one of the traditions in the Old Religion, taught her of the days when followers celebrated Nature as the High Holy Mystery. During rituals, ecstasy was experienced and enjoyed by participants who believed that just as heaven and earth made love, so too could humans join their bodies, minds, spirits, and souls to the Great Mystery. Sexual, life-affirming energy was considered the reservoir of creativity.

Now in the twentieth century, Stephanie has a master's degree in counseling psychology from the University of San Francisco, as well as certificates in hypnotherapy and massage. In her commitment to being a messenger, she often travels to professional conferences throughout North America to present papers on shamanistic sexology, providing a voice for almost forgotten songs sung by ancestors centuries ago.

She is also very familiar with sex surrogacy, which on the surface bares resemblance to her role as a FireWoman, a teacher of spiritual sexuality. Philosophically though, sex surrogacy and Fire Medicine come from very different orientations. Sex surrogacy is based on medical concepts of sexual dysfunction, all within a pathology model. Fire Medicine views the physical, the energetic, and the spiritual as an integrated whole; sexuality is at the center of personal development and metamorphosis.

Stephanie has been deeply drawn to be a bicultural messenger of a Native American Fire Medicine tradition. Though most mainstream sexologists accept her as a colleague, she sometimes struggles to find ways to present her concept of spiritual sexuality to a general public that would often rather be titillated than enlightened. This has become her challenge. She has chosen a shamanic warrior's path, and, as she writes: "A warrior never wages war on others. The battle is always fought internally."

The FireWoman

by

Stephanie Rainbow Lightning Elk

All things are connected. Whatever befalls the earth, befalls the children of the earth.

Chief Seattle

Medicine, as used by Native Americans, is that which connects us to the Great Mystery, to the All-That-Is. When we use our Medicine for healthy purposes, we awaken our personal powers and gain knowledge.

Medicine can be the way one listens, the way one knows how to help others in times of stress or trouble. Medicine can be a sense of humor, an expertise in electronics, an awareness of subtle energies. It can be a way of teaching yoga, an aspect of parenting, the ability to share openly and honestly. Medicine can be an artistic talent or a way of being a friend. Medicine can be a way of utilizing sexual energy for healing purposes.

My Medicine was awakened and expanded with my studies of Earth-centered spirituality and my introduction to Native American ways, especially through three *metis* (of mixed ancestry) Cherokee Medicine Men: Grandpa Robert, Keetowah, and Harley SwiftDeer.

I had never seen a Cherokee like Grandpa Robert, a tall white-haired man of immense presence. I could feel the sexual life-force energy pulsating throughout his body whenever I was near him. He lived to the age of ninety-eight years, fathering a son, one of many children, just prior to passing on. The scent of the woods, giant redwood trees and mosses, exuded from his sturdy frame. Grandpa Robert initiated me into the beginnings of shamanism. I had not been consciously aware of tapping into other energies, although I had experienced unusual events.

Whenever I spent time with Grandpa Robert, his carved serpent staff accompanied him. I remember at a particular gathering we were attending, the moon had revealed herself as a tiny crescent in the brilliant sky. That twilight evening he turned his full attention on me, although there were others in the smudge-filled room. (We had burned cedar, sage, and lavender to cleanse the area, to bless our time together, and to center ourselves.) His large, deerlike eyes were of a color I could not recognize in the moment. "You take this shaman's staff for a while, young lady," he quietly insisted. As my small hands wrapped around the twisted stick, I was transported in my mind to another place and another time.

In my mind's eye we were sitting around a campfire, drumming and chanting in harmony. Ceremonies and rituals honoring nature and the passage of time brought images of sweet childhood expectations fulfilled. My eyes closed tightly. I wanted to feel with all of my body's instincts—to smell the sweat of my skin, to taste the churning of saliva as the chant rolled out of my mouth, to hear the sound of the fire crackling and the drums beating, to feel our heartbeats as one, to see the glow of energy dancing around our bodies.

The power of Grandpa Robert's serpent staff had carried me deeply into a memory of other times. I took another look at the naturally twisted stick held between my hands, grasped between my legs. Two serpent's bodies wrapped around each other making up the length of the staff, signifying Snake Medicine, the most powerful of healing energies, the ability to shed the old and transform to the new. I looked into the ruby eyes of the snake heads and wondered how he used this instrument.

My awareness shifted from my inner imaginings to the outer world of the living room as others in the room began to get up and leave. It was time for Grandpa to go. He winked at me as he reached for his staff, and I laughed to myself as I imagined him making the stick come alive.

The living room that we sat in was Keetowah's. Keetowah was a small, wiry, birdlike man, also of Cherokee descent. He was known throughout the San Francisco Bay Area as the Crystal Godfather and was a master concerning the energies and healing properties of crystals. Keetowah was in his seventies, although he counted his time here according to seasons and not length of years. Grandpa Robert said Keetowah was just a kid.

Keetowah taught me about the old Cherokee ways, though I found it difficult to be around him because he chain-smoked Kool King cigarettes and coughed spasmodically between drags. Due to his smoking habit I learned how to deal with "environmental tyrants." He taught me how to master my sense of smell and use my vision in a way that would narrow my focus. By doing this I only took in to my body what was necessary and determined by my choice. At the time I did not realize that he was teaching me aspects of shamanism. Little did I know that I would be asked to create a sexual healing ceremony with this elder a few years later.

In 1984 I traveled to the Ojai Foundation, near Santa Barbara, California, for a month-long event. Here, at this center which is a gathering place for scholars, scientists, shamans, Buddhist monks, counselors, and spiritual teachers, I attended a program titled "Awakening the Dream: The Way of the Warrior." Joan Halifax, Harley SwiftDeer, and R. D. Laing were the leaders of what was to become a transformative event for me.

Meeting Harley SwiftDeer inspired me to commit myself to a study of Native American spirituality, a path with heart. This fortuitous meeting would also lead me into a more complex and deeper study of shamanism combined with spiritual sexuality teachings. I wanted to learn all that I could from SwiftDeer when I heard him say, "Wars will stop when women and men stop the wars between themselves in the bedroom." The war between my male and female self inside was raging; I wanted to reach a peaceful agreement within myself and externally with my partners.

I left the conference a changed person, now committed to awakening my own dream: I knew what I wanted to do, I knew what I had to do.

I felt deeply drawn to seek out this coyote shaman I knew as SwiftDeer. In Native American traditions the coyote is the trickster who offers us ways to laugh at ourselves, especially when we think it is important to be proper, special, or serious. Coyote shamanism encourages us to be clear, strong, humorous, and fun loving as we meet life-and-death challenges.

Months passed. I attempted to find SwiftDeer no matter where

I was working. On a journey to Hawaii I was successful late one night. "It's midnight," I thought, "surely, he'll answer his phone." What would he tell me? "Quodoushka is what you're looking for," he suggested. "How do you spell that?" I asked. He could not tell me, although he attempted in a frustrated manner. I recall thinking, "How can he teach something he cannot spell?" Of course, I had a typical linear, Western point of view; but that would change over time with knowledge, practice, and ceremony.

Our conversation that night lead me to a Quodoushka workshop in Los Angeles. I knew this was where I would begin to confront my rifts between sexuality, sensuality, and spirituality.

SwiftDeer is of mixed heritage. His father is Irish, and his mother is Cherokee. Acknowledged as a shaman and healer, he is on the Council of Twisted Hairs, whose members seek knowledge from all cultures. Known as "braids of truths," their teachings have usually been passed on orally. SwiftDeer teaches the Sweet Medicine Sun Dance path of "right relationship" (correct alignment) with all the worlds: plant, mineral, animal, human, and spirit. As a master storyteller, he weaves his personal experiences into the teachings. Adding humor and compassion along the way, he has the capacity to explore as deeply as one is willing to go.

SwiftDeer, under the guidance of his elders, chose to bring out the *Chuluaqui-Quodoushka (CHOO-la-kway Kwuh-DOE-shka)* teachings and ceremonies. These teachings challenge sexual repression, offering sexual knowledge and freedom. At his discretion he began to teach and train a select group of people to carry these once secret and oral traditions to the public. I wanted to be one of those select few to learn about *Fire Medicine*, the path of spiritual sexuality.

Sexuality teachings during rites of passage from childhood to adulthood form the foundation of the Quodoushka way. In most indigenous cultures, rites of passage include puberty rituals, vision quests to seek knowledge and personal power, and purification ceremonies such as sweat lodges that accompany the reentry of the child into the culture as an adult. Western European culture is lacking in ceremonies that honor the passage of time. Apparent as low self-esteem, especially in the area of sexuality, our young people do not experience receiving respect. Most of us have been shamed, and guilt and fear diminish our ability to feel pleasure. We have been taught that pleasure is to be avoided unless it is the reward after long hours of work. Indeed, in some circumstances, sexual play has become work. Somehow, we have acquired the distorted idea that we must try harder to reach deeper, we must study and experience more until we have mastered transcendence.

Modern society has lost the mysteries that help frame important life questions. Long ago, spiritual rites were part of the cultures of ancient Greece, Africa, Egypt, and other parts of Europe. Pagans (named by the Christians, referring to those who were not Christian or Jewish) celebrated nature with rituals and ceremonies to mark the seasonal changes. The sacred union of heaven and earth, the essence of cosmic sexuality, was honored. Lacking these rituals and rites of passage, our Western culture feels soulless. We have lost our connection to the true reality: Nature.

During the Los Angeles workshop I was reunited with a natural view of the world. I learned the comprehensive system of the Medicine Wheel, an ancient spiritual tool and concept found in most indigenous cultures. Also known as a sacred hoop, circle, or mandala, the Medicine Wheel teaches us to experience our lives via a nonlinear perspective, similar in concept to a holographic thought process without beginning or end. We travel the circle, gaining new perspectives from each vantage point as we continue to pass through all the positions over and over again.

Learning and practicing aspects of sexuality from this perspective gave me a chance to understand myself in a profound way. When I first heard the basic teaching of the Medicine Wheel, I knew that I had found a home. In the South (water), we honor our emotions. In the West (earth), we honor our bodies. In the North (air), we honor our minds. In the East (fire), we honor our spirits. And in the Center (the void), we honor our sexual catalyst-life-force energy. The Medicine Wheel way of the Chuluaqui-Quodoushka teachings empowers divine connection through the life-force energy that we call sexual.

I knew that healing the rifts between spirituality and sexuality would be a powerful political statement. With this integration I learned how to be sexually responsible, confident, and empowered. Freedom to make my own choices was essential now, and I wanted to educate others to this comprehensive system.

However, I had to take a break, and so I returned to my job assisting a brilliant plant breeder doing research in the tomato and cotton fields. We were trying to find a better, healthier way to grow food and clothing. With dirt under my fingernails, I walked the land, communing with the soil, the water, the sun, and the plants. It felt good to be in touch with the earth.

Still the teachings and ceremonies of the Sweet Medicine Sun Dance path called to me. I would dream about rituals that I wanted to participate in, and the Quodoushka teachings inspired my thoughts and behaviors even in the tomato fields. Consequently, for three years I attended a Quodoushka seminar every month—sometimes as participant, sometimes as facilitator, sometimes as staff teacher.

By 1986 I decided to apprentice to SwiftDeer. I gave him Medicine gifts of tobacco and a Medicine blanket along with my desire to learn as much as possible. Within time, after long hours of intense ceremonies, I was initiated into the tradition of a FireWoman. Practicing as a FireWoman was to became the way that I could share this Medicine Wheel knowledge with others.

Among some of the clans of the Cherokee, FireWomen and FireMen were chosen by a Council of Grandmothers, women of wisdom and knowledge. If there was an abuse of power, then one answered to the Council of Grandmothers. Years of training for FirePeople included Medicine Wheel teachings, rites of passage, techniques utilizing breathing practices and energy vortices within and surrounding the body, as well as knowledge of genital anatomy types and sexual preferences. Sexual role-playing with the Lover's Mask Medicine Wheel had to be mastered. (The term *lover's mask* symbolizes the personas or ways that we consciously or unconsciously interact with our partner(s) to convey our sexual needs, wants, and desires.)

The Firebreath Orgasm was taught and practiced as a way to generate self-healing. This full-body orgasm that was produced through breathing, visualization, and pelvic movements without any genital stimulation offered a way to experience natural healing and a state of bliss. Orgasm was and is understood as a powerful healing mechanism; types and levels of orgasm were studied and practiced. Rituals were encouraged as a way to achieve harmony. Initiator and initiate could experience transcendence.

Within this tradition, there is no hierarchy or power structure; instead, there is an exchange of energies, a "dance of mirrors." We learn that we are reflections of each other: where you are in your desire to "grow up," I once was. Practitioners avoid ego gratification. They sponsor "love" as they facilitate a natural flow of energy through one's whole being. Here, the love is more of a spiritual nature than the romantic kind fostered in the everyday modern world.

In the olden days a young person was given a choice of working with a FirePerson who helped educate and awaken sexuality in harmony with spirituality. In today's world, adult initiates come to me for the same ceremony. Yesterday, Medicine gifts were exchanged; today, money and sometimes Medicine gifts are exchanged. All represent exchanges of energy. The FirePerson expends power and energy to accomplish the Quodoushka ceremonies; gifts are given to balance this exchange. This is not a concept of commerce; this is a concept of renewal and energy balance.

My initiates are men and women (ages twenty to eighty) seeking a way to heal from the sexual wounding of our culture. Each initiate desires feeling comfortable and confident with his or her sexuality. Today, my initiates are mostly males who bear the brunt of the burden of distorted and repressed sexuality. Usually feeling uncomfortable in their bodies, they are often at war with themselves. Their social persona is overripe before their inner one has grown up. In losing the contours of this persona, each yearns to be reunited with their bodies and their intimacy. By finding the integrity of their natural selves, they begin a reintegration of body and soul, mind and spirit.

When an initiate arrives at my house, a place that is a museum of handmade ceremonial objects and tools of sacred power that have been gifted to me, he or she enters another world. This world assists in their transformation. I have made my house into a space where there is respect and honor for all that surrounds us. Each item, holding a sacred energy, is arranged in a way that honors natural and alchemical laws of universal energy and harmony.

Here, in my warm, firelit house, is a place wherein they can shed their old skins. "I want to feel totally comfortable with my sexuality," each petitions in various ways. Most have not experienced much intimacy in their lives, either with themselves or with another.

My initiates and I explore the causes of their sexual misconceptions, traumas, shame, insecurities, ignorance, guilt, fears, needs, wants, desires, dreams, relationships, and experiences. Quietly, gently, each finding ourself in the other, we touch and talk. With our developing "love" we create the sacred in our relationship. We take the time to develop trust. This is no different from a relationship that happens by chance. We know there will be a beginning, a middle, and an end to this story we create. The wheel continues to spin even as we follow our paths.

First and foremost, I teach each initiate how to be present in his or her body, how to become aware of the sexual energy that moves through the body. I use breathing practices to activate conscious awareness, focused attention, and the potential for expanded experiences of ecstasy. A type of massage called body imprint removal begins to recondition and reeducate the body and mind.

We are then ready to understand the energy vortices inside the body, outside the body, as well as the body as a vortex unto itself. In Tantra these vortices are known as chakras; in Quodoushka they are called chuluas, of which there are ten centers that are activated.

As the initiate and I begin to merge our energy centers, we realize that we are entering into a conscious awareness of where our sexual feelings and sensations are flowing smoothly and where they are not. We relearn how to play, with pleasure. Feelings of communion, trust, and personal power unfold.

In of all this, I am first a believer. I believe in a context that allows us to sponsor love for one another, not as gods or goddesses, not as role players in a romantic drama, but as humans who crumble and fall, only to get up again to continue the quest for honorable friendship and companionship.

Whenever I am with my initiates, I enter an altered state of consciousness, enabling me to "read" the energy in their bodies. I determine where this energy is blocked in their bodies, and how it may be released. None of this works unless our relationship is grounded in trust. I engage in understanding the fires of their sexual thoughts, feelings, and desires. I teach each to bring that fire within to full flame.

Following the Quodoushka tradition brings a new awareness of beauty and pleasure in the initiate. As we progress, my feelings intensify, and I feel I am witnessing a rebirth. The initiate's self, hidden for so many years, emerges. I am privileged to be a part of this metamorphosis.

When our time together is complete, as determined by the initiate, we review our work together. Each, in various ways, sums up his or her experience. I am surprised at how often the same theme emerges. Many of them say, "It was different— it was not what I expected. I came for techniques, and I got those, but I received experiences that helped me grow up." Many of them say they wished they had received these teachings when they were younger, at the age of puberty.

❦

My initiates come from various walks of life, seeking these teachings and ceremonies for various reasons.

The idea of growing into a lusty, powerful, and responsible sexual persona captivated one young woman in her early forties. A principal of a high school, she was overweight and felt somewhat ashamed at achieving so much in lieu of maintaining a family life for herself. She came to me to learn how to balance her life between work, family, and pleasure. Of course, pleasure had been left out. Carrying the extra weight on her body was preventing her from being fully sexual and powerful at the same time. We explored how she could best utilize her sexual energy to catalyze her becoming the person she visioned, physically, emotionally, and spiritually.

Some come to me seeking a way to activate their sexual energy as a tool for healing. A practicing chiropractor consulted me for this reason. He knew that if he could be consciously aware and in charge of his sexual energy, he could transmit this as a healing force through his hands. He did not want to sponsor this energy as a turn-on;

instead he wanted to be totally aware of his life-force energy as a way to facilitate movement of energy for others.

One initiate came to me, drawn by the historical content of the Quodoushka teachings. He was a tall, long-muscled, tanned, aqua-eyed Navy SEAL.

Owing to cultural conditioning and the attendant lack of experience of eroticism, he held judgments about his body that were founded on shame. Consequently, his sexuality manifested in unhealthy ways. At twenty-six he had a history of relationships with women who had been abused, physically or emotionally, and sometimes sexually. He wanted to learn more about healing energy for himself and for others. In contrast to his training in Western medicine, he wanted to understand dis-ease from a holistic perspective.

His training as a Navy SEAL, medic, and combat photographer had created limits in his ability to understand sexual energy when used in the context of healing. He also wanted to enhance his sex life in a personal way—relaxed with open eyes. He wanted to learn how to receive. He wanted to release his adventurous spirit in the bedroom, not on the killing fields.

Lying on the bed, I taught him how to synchronize his breathing rhythm with mine. We listened for the sounds of our heartbeats, the sound of the drums, wild chanting in our heads. The smoke of cedar, sage, and lavender cleansed the environment and the energy fields around our bodies.

With eyes half closed, softly focused, we slowed down. Our sensations came alive. I could see the pulsation of his erotic energy, like an electric field of color around his body. I told him to feel it as a color or sound coursing through his body, looping it, and circulating it. Sitting on top of him, my hands forming a healing symbol over his heart, my tupuli and his tipili (the Quodoushka words for male and female genitals) touched and merged energetically as one—physical intercourse was not necessary for this cosmic dance. Both of us feeling the pull of strong sexual energy, our breathing synchronized naturally.

Directing him to look into my eyes, I began to make strong sounds of pleasure. My pelvis began rocking back and forth as I contracted my vulva muscles to increase the sexual energy. Then I instructed him to follow my breathing, listen to my sounds, and match what I was doing. We entered an altered state of awareness, acutely sensitive to each other's passion. My hands glided across his body, directing his erotic energy all over him. I guided him to send this energy to wherever he needed it to go, into his body, mind, soul, or spirit, and on into his dreams and desires.

Our experience together created more questions for him. He needed the goad of tough questions to enliven the quest for truthful answers. This young surfer, scuba diver, writer, and craftsman of the arrows he hunted with, wanted to increase his personal knowledge. He needed to understand energy as life-giving whereas previously he had used this same erotic energy to kill.

Serving in El Salvador, he had killed, by his reckoning, fourteen people. He had learned how to manipulate his sexual energy to protect himself, which meant killing others to survive. He was one of the few men I knew willing to admit that over time the killing was a turn-on for him. Power surged through his body whenever he pulled the trigger. At times when he was successful with his mission, he reported feeling invincible. It was a kind of erotic frenzy: bullets whizzing all around, men falling as he aimed his machine gun, and the beginnings of an erection growing. He had been afraid to tell this part of his experience to anyone previously.

His military time up, he had traveled to Alaska. He needed to be in the wild, open space of nature at its best. Eagles graced his vision as each day passed, and he began to forgive himself for his military career. He wanted to come to terms with his deeds of killing. An Apache Medicine Man there took him on as an apprentice.

Together they did ceremony to put the past behind him. Guided by the Apache Medicine Man, he was taught how to sing the death songs for those fourteen people. He prayed and sent up smoke in the pipe ceremony. Feeling as destroyed as his victims, he began to put himself back together.

The pipe ceremony opens the door to other worlds and the Great Mystery, to the powers of nature and beyond. A tradition with many Native American groups, the pipe ceremony is one of the most powerful ways of connecting with the Great Mystery. It is not a plaything; it is both sacred symbol and tool. It is used only during times that require great introspection and clear purpose.

Here was a killer and a seeker, an American warrior as best he knew how to be. But something was not right. He wanted to find his way back to his heart and his innocence. Often times when he would experience his sexual energy rising, he would have flashbacks to the times of killing. We spent time in pipe ceremony dealing with his flashbacks and creating a new memory for his body and mind.

As we practiced eye-to-eye energy-merging rituals, he was able to create intimacy with me in a way that had been usually difficult for him. With his sexual energy more clearly directed and more lovingly expressed, his will was strengthened. His lack of properly directed will had been noticeable in his potbellied, loose-skinned stomach. As his will strengthened, his abdominal muscles became more toned. He was less subject to illness and the loss of vitality from sluggish, blocked energy.

His inner life in balance with his outer life, flowing with primal life force, he felt more confident. He began to find a way to be at peace with himself and his past. Playful, like an otter, he gained a new spirit of adventure. He began to envision a new purpose for his life. He learned that, in this path of shamanism, a warrior never wages war on others. The battle is always fought internally.

❧

Originally, Fire Medicine was taught to young people as they passed through puberty rituals. Later in life, if a person had an illness or life-threatening condition, then a Phoenix FirePerson could facilitate the possibility of a return to good health.

Within the Chuluaqui-Quodoushka tradition, the Phoenix FirePerson is an initiate in the advanced practices of spiritual sexuality. This Medicine Person is required to demonstrate an advanced level of sexual healing. Opportunities for the Phoenix FirePerson came unexpectedly as tribal members required assistance. When someone showed up with a life-threatening problem, Fire Medicine was utilized to catalyze self-healing, effect remission, or restore health. For the one who sought these healing energies, the intent was to extend life for as long as necessary to complete a commitment to a purpose. The sexual healing ceremony done with Keetowah years later gave me the opportunity to test my abilities before I could be called a Phoenix.

The Phoenix practices brought me into a greater appreciation for ritual and ceremony. I was reminded of my early days when being raised as Catholic had revealed the mysteries of spirituality. I was aware of unusual energy experiences within the sanctity of the church. A place of candlelight and stained glass, where the Holy Mother held a special place, and saints from old watched over the sacred objects of long ago, I recall feeling as if I was splendid also. Lights and colors danced amid the incense haze, forming halos and crowns, affirming the presence of divine energy. Certain items were considered sacred, not to be touched by a thin-as-a-stick, tow-haired child. I wanted to touch them all, but the priests held the power over the special objects.

In the shamanism path I have chosen I can now participate in not only working with sacred objects but also in creating them. Through creating my own Medicine shields, leather tobacco bags, crystal healing wands, and other special tools, I hold the power to use them. Now chanting, drumming, and the burning of smudge to cleanse and create a ceremonial place take me to the same special place where once the High Mass and cherubic altar boys swinging the censer did.

Now the sweat lodge rituals have taught me how to pray in a new way, how to honor my body as sacred, and how to walk lightly on the Earth. Vision quests and ceremonies that place me in nature for days at a time have given me clarity to understand my purpose. Going without food and water for three days while dancing back and forth to the "tree of life" in the Dreamer's Sun Dance have taught me compassion and have given me the courage and stamina to continue being different. Now shamanism resides at the core of my being.

When I am a guide, showing a path of spirit, I am a FireWoman. My sensuality is a deep river. By claiming this wild, lusty river of my self, I feel my life's reasons for being. I am strong and vulnerable at the same time. All of nature lives in me. I am earth spirit, water spirit, air spirit, fire spirit.

I dance full circle around the Medicine Wheel with grace and joy.

For all my relations,
Stephanie Rainbow Lightning Elk

KATHRYN

❦

THE NURSE

Introduction to

KATHRYN

Kathryn is her pseudonym—witch-hunts are still a reality. She is a nurse, has a graduate degree in human sexuality, and currently teaches at a major American university. Revealing her name could result in termination of her medical career.

I first met Kathryn when she attended my sensate therapy training program while she was working on her graduate degree in human sexuality. This hands-on training program for sex therapists and educators presented a wide range of sensate focus techniques, such as relaxation exercises, sensual bathing, sensual feeding, gentle massage, and other mind-and-body nurturing methods, similar to the Secret Garden Ceremony and what is taught in sex surrogate courses. Since these students were to become or already were practicing sexologists, I included genital massage, oral lovemaking techniques, pelvic bathing, as well as G-spot, prostate, and anal massage. The basic guideline always was: if it is pleasurable for the recipient, you are doing it correctly. Unfortunately, such an approach is often antithetical to mainstream medical training, where *clinical* and *ethical* sometimes actually mean *painful* and *impersonal*, at least in practice if not in theory.

Any therapeutic process resulting in a pleasurable sexual experience—for either "the client" or "the therapist"—especially if genital or anal touching is included, could easily provoke a flurry of castigations: sexual abuse, sexual harassment, molestation, prostitution. A practitioner of the healing arts risks the loss of licensure and a career. Should the recipient later reinterpret a positive occurrence as negative, litigation looms as a possibility. So when Kathryn, visiting me in the hospital where I lay paralyzed from a broken neck, told me about her experience with Jonnie, a quadriplegic who had spent his entire adult life of over thirty years on a hospital ward, I felt it essential his story be included here. His life seemed very relevant to my own and anyone else's caught up in the sometimes dehumanizing system of medical care.

With Jonnie, Kathryn went far beyond the call of duty, focusing on pleasure, being clinical without being painful and impersonal. Stepping outside pseudo-ethical mandates, she embraced the sexual and nurtured the spiritual with Jonnie and became a healer in the truest sense. Her sincerity and her willingness to risk was compassionate and honorable, a model for what a healing professional *can* be.

THE NURSE

by

Kathryn

When I met Jonnie, my new patient, the first thing I noticed was his warm, radiant smile. He had short black curly hair and an amputated leg. His body was paralyzed with no movement and sensation from his shoulders to his toes.

From the age of eighteen, when he was suddenly paralyzed from an automobile accident, Jonnie had lived in institutions for a total of thirty years. Nurses, doctors, and physical therapists made up his social life during his late teens, early, and middle adult years. All of his family members had died, and he no longer had outside visitors.

I became Jonnie's primary nurse, which meant I was assigned to him on a regular basis. We felt at ease with each other instantly. He was a quadriplegic; thus it was my job to assist him in almost all of his bodily functions: to move, bathe, dress, undress, eat, urinate, and defecate.

Since Jonnie never left the hospital, the outside world came to him through his caregivers. Jonnie's social and sexual development had come to an abrupt halt with his accident. So when I told him that I was also a graduate student in sexology, a wide range of questions poured forth. "How do people feel when they are in love?" "What do they say to each other when they are in love or sexually attracted to each other?" "How does the body feel when in love and sexually aroused?" "What can my body feel?" "How can I have more physical sensations and sexual feelings?" I answered what I knew and was honest with what I didn't know.

Jonnie's greatest desire was to experience sensation in his mostly paralyzed, numb body, something to give him feedback that he was physically alive. His motivation was very strong when he asked for my assistance. There was a potential problem however. If I helped him, I could lose my job were the explorations perceived by hospital administrators or coworkers as being in any way sexual.

Never having attempted this type of education/therapy before and because each person's potential is different, I really did not know what his body could experience. Drawing on my backgrounds in sexology and in meditation, I felt two approaches might be best. The first, known as sensate focus, would be simply to focus, to concentrate, to be aware of the physical sensations of taste, touch, smell, sound, and sight occurring during an activity. The second method was to be open to an attitude, a feeling of unconditional love. I explained that awakening the love that has no conditions, boundaries, or limits is a love that is available to all human beings. Jonnie began focusing on unconditional loving thoughts centered in his heart area. I invited him to visualize white light saturated with love filling every cell of his body and continuing to radiate beyond his skin surface.

We decided to focus fully on the activities already being experienced in his daily life. Eating became a new experience as his attention was drawn to the food during mealtime. There was the sight of ripe, red, juicy, sweet strawberries topped with whipped cream, and the sharp smell of pickles. There was the sweetness of chocolate frosting swirling over his tongue, and the crunch of fresh, firm carrot sticks. The key was to appreciate the aliveness of the senses.

After food is processed by the body, the remains have to be expelled, and quadriplegics do not have the ability to activate the peristaltic wave of the intestines on their own. In order to produce a bowel movement, a caregiver must stimulate the nerves in the anus with an inserted finger, a process termed *digital stimulation*. Hospital protocol calls for a minimum of five minutes or whatever time it takes to empty the bowel of its contents. From my experience, five minutes never had much effect on my patients in regards to stimulating the undulant wave; it always required a good twenty to thirty minutes. An effective bowel movement is absolutely crucial to a spinal cord injured person because a full bowel could cause a condition called *dysreflexia*. This comes on suddenly from irritations such as a full bladder, full bowel, or skin pain. If dysreflexia is not relieved quickly, high blood pressure can cause further disabilities from a stroke. Death can also be a consequence. Every quadriplegic quickly learns that a good emptying of the bowel is paramount to staying alive, while a poor emptying can be life threatening.

With a positive attitude toward our body, particularly the anus and prostate gland, our brain will usually interpret stimulation from this area as pleasurable. When receiving digital stimulation, most people recovering from a spinal cord injury are not encouraged to focus on any sensation. For the purpose of our exploration, I encouraged Jonnie to focus on any and all sensations during the bowel program. I sometimes played soothing music to help create a sense of calmness and to help the oftentimes spasmodic muscles to relax. Since early childhood, most of us have been taught that eliminating feces should be done as quickly as possible, as unconsciously as possible, and with a feeling of disgust. When children are taught attitudes of fear, avoidance, and disdain in connection with learning bowel control, emotional scars are left in the psyche, which poisons their feelings for their bodies and affects sexual and general health. Some spiritual work is definitely needed in changing these attitudes.

I stressed the sacredness of every cell in Jonnie's body, which included the cells that were no longer needed and must be released to keep the body healthy and alive. I also stressed the sacredness of all sensations wherever the sensations existed. We were on a journey exploring where undiscovered sensations might exist, and we hoped to find pleasurable physical feelings along the way.

After thirty years of being unconscious of his sensations in his anus and prostate, Jonnie discovered that he not only had physical sensations, but that they were indeed pleasurable. He was delighted, after such a long time of living in his body with so few sensations, to find a treasure hidden in his depths. In order to amplify the sensations, I suggested that he focus his attention on his breath in addition to the other physical sensations. As Jonnie drew in a deep breath on the inhalation, fully inflating his upper lobes of his lungs, and then relaxing with the exhalation, the intensity of the sensation began to build. His entire body began to sense a different awareness. Even though he did not have a name for it, he was becoming aware of his ability to build his own life force. The deeper he breathed, the more extensive were his sensations. Jonnie's daily bowel program of digital stimulation became his meditation time—a time when he was unfolding the mysteries of becoming more alive.

❧

The shower room was about the only place a patient could find any privacy. Jonnie loved long showers. Even though he couldn't feel from his nipples down any sensations from touch, he enjoyed my playfulness as I sprayed water over his skin from head to toe, soaped and scrubbed his body, and briskly dried him off with a towel. The shower was the place where he felt safe in breathing more deeply, allowing his breath to carry a sound. I encouraged him to focus on any and all sensations. While receiving a shampoo, Jonnie loved having his head vigorously massaged and scratched. He felt new tingly sensations in the skin covering his ears, face, neck, and shoulders. Some bath times were filled with laughter and play, while others were quiet and serene.

One day in the shower room, I suggested to Jonnie that he move his shoulders in such a way that his arms could stimulate his chest and nipple area. At my suggestion, he closed his eyes to decrease the visual stimulation and to allow more attention for his sense of touch. He soon entered into a very deep, quiet space as he focused on his breath, sensations, and love feelings. As I massaged his entire body with soap and water, I spoke softly to him, telling him how powerful every breath carrying the energy of love was in awakening his body. I whispered how relaxed and gentle his face looked, as he opened his heart to a deeper appreciation of his body, exactly the way it was in that moment of time. Inhaling and exhaling in unison with Jonnie's, I focused my attention on activating and intensifying my heart energy of unconditional love.

As the energy streamed out my fingertips, I could feel tingles and warmth in my arms and hands. His breathing quickened in pace as I washed his soft penis. When I rinsed his pelvic floor and anal area with the water nozzle, I noticed rapid eye movement under his closed eyelids. Jonnie was experiencing something very new and different. The rapid eye movement lasted for about a minute, then a peaceful stillness enveloped the whole room.

When Jonnie's eyes opened, he immediately asked, "What happened?"

I asked him the same question. He recalled that he was drifting in space, breathing, and melting into a sea of love. He felt connected to everything in the universe. Suddenly, wavelike pulsations had streamed down his entire body, down *both* legs, and out his toes— electrical impulses vibrating from both his physical and "phantom" leg. His "energy body," which interpenetrates and surrounds the physical body, was obviously intact and included both legs.

With a broad smile I said, "I believe you just had an orgasm."

Jonnie's unexpected and yet very welcome orgasm opened up all kinds of questions. First of all, he wanted to know how he could have an orgasm without an erection or ejaculation. I told him that there are numerous types of orgasms. An ejaculatory orgasm is just one type. I explained that he apparently had a type of orgasm called by various writers an energetic, metasexual, total body, or cosmic orgasm. Whatever the name, I was sure that he had experienced an orgasm. Love, breath, and movement had unleashed his orgasmic energy.

This wondrous gift of life needed to be kept a secret from everyone. Sadly, Jonnie did not have any friends to share this momentous event, and he knew that to tell any of the hospital staff could lead to repercussions. Jonnie hoped, however, that maybe he could somehow have another experience similar to this one. That dream would never be realized.

Soon after his orgasmic experience, Jonnie learned that he had developed an untreatable cancer. The outcome was clear; his physical body would soon stop functioning and death would come. We talked about the meaning of life and death, how some people experienced those last few days and hours before the last breath.

One night one of the nurses called me at home to inform me that Jonnie appeared to be in his final hours. I immediately went in to be with him. When I entered the room, the first thing I noticed was his big, wide open, terrified eyes. His breathing was labored, like a person going through a frightening experience. He was conscious and aware of my presence, but not conversant other than with a yes or no. I could see and feel how frightened he was, in a room all by himself—dying.

I told him that I would stay with him and would not leave until he had finally let go of his body. I gently stroked his head, face, neck, and shoulders and began softly speaking into his ears. I knew that the sense of hearing was one of the last to function, so I kept talking. I talked about his life force not needing this physical body anymore. The hours ticked by in the darkness and quietness of the night. His eyes were closed and his breathing became peaceful and rhythmic. I reassured him that he could let go and merge with all in the universe, just like he did the day he had his orgasm. I reminded him of that life-force energy that had streamed through his body—that life energy that sometimes has form and sometimes does not.

Jonnie and I had talked about white light before, visualizing it entering and flooding his body. Now it was time for him to merge with the white light in a way he had never done before. I reassured him that his spirit, his body, his mind, his total being was unconditional love. I stayed with him throughout the night, supporting his consciousness in being as comfortable as possible as it separated from the physical form it had inhabited for over fifty years. His one orgasmic experience had come to him as what seemed to be a preparation for the biggest letting go that we as humans get to experience.

His breaths became more shallow and fewer in number; a look of deep relaxation and serenity appeared upon his face. I encouraged him to invite family members who had passed out of their physical bodies years before to assist him in his transition and welcome his spirit.

Jonnie's body became totally motionless, quiet, and serene. There was not another breath, as the soft light of dawn began to penetrate the black veil of night.

women of the night

Women of the Light

Conclusion:
From
Sexual Stereotype
to Archetype

by

Kenneth Ray Stubbs, Editor

Her eyes connect with mine, actually gazing past
mine into my soul, perhaps even into the soul of the
universe. Her face, far from expressionless, conveys

she is transcendent even while her sensual, sexual essence flows freely as a river within her. Though I see only her head, throat, and shoulders, I know she is grounded in her pelvis and thighs, her feet planted firmly on the Earth; I sense she walks in grace and beauty. Her headdress suggests she is devoted to her sacred path; the halo indicates she is energetically evolved beyond ordinary human capabilities. Her palm and fingers of one hand held up facing me in symbolic gesture say, "Be at peace." And the egg encompassed by her fingers—she does not hold it, she reveals it, for she is the messenger. The egg is enlightened birth and life, knowledge and wisdom. They are available to me, to all who wish to receive, but I must choose to extend my open hand and open heart to receive the gift.

In my more contemplative moments I know *she* is more than a she—I know that *she* is me, her appearance being of a form that my mind might interpret, might begin to find recognizable meaning as I in deep desire seek to once again be in at-one-ment with Source.

This is what I envision when I look into the painting of Mary Magdalene, Christendom's ultimate sacred prostitute, on the cover of this book.[1]

Whether Mary Magdalene was a repentant whore turned nun,

---

[1] This painting by Richard Stodart is based on a black-and-white image appearing on a picture postcard given by a nun to Nancy Qualls-Corbett, Ph.D., when she visited the Cathedral of Mary Magdalene in Jerusalem doing research on her groundbreaking book *The Sacred Prostitute*.

or a sanctified saintly courtesan, or Jesus's favorite or only lover, or Jesus's closest disciple, or a combination of these we will never know. Fact has become legend, in fact, many legends; and now we tell the legends because this *she* is an archetype, the sacred prostitute archetype.

Modern psychology applies the adjective *archetypal* when some "thing" in the world comes to symbolize something far more profound than the historical fact. A person such as Mary Magdalene, an event such as a war of liberation, a sound such as the Eastern chant "Om," a visual form such as a circle—these "external" symbols resonate deep within our psyche, our unconsciousness, our soul. They pull on our attention, we are drawn to them...and we often don't really know why. They resonate within us because they mirror back to us some meaningful aspect of our innate self.

The women of the light in this book are contemporary human beings serving a significant sexual function in our culture: we see them waking in grace and beauty on a sacred sexual path. Following Jungian analyst Nancy Qualls-Corbett's perspective that the sacred prostitute is the physical embodiment of the archetypal goddess of love, I have suggested throughout this book that we view these women of the light and their functions through the lenses of an archetype; otherwise, most of us would have only a stereotype to contemplate sexual service compensated with money.

The common stereotype of the modern prostitute is that the practitioner is female, the client is male. The prostitute is often a drug addict and always a victim: oppressive economic conditions or oppressive men have forced her against her will into this occupation, and she finds the sexual service neither meaningful nor pleasurable.

Doubtless throughout history there have been and still are many individuals who fit this stereotype. The women of the light in this book clearly do not. All of them are of service to both genders (and there are men of the light who do likewise). To call these visionaries *victims* would be erroneous; they are unusually self-reliant and psychologically independent; they have made conscious choices, often responding to a calling from their innermost voice. Nor does *drug addict* apply. One might even argue whether *prostitute* is applicable to most of the women of the light here. Several of them neither identify with nor embrace the label, *sacred* or otherwise. Nonetheless, in most localities, should the legal system decide to arrest and prosecute, some form of prostitution would likely be the charge.

Some scholars distinguish between a *secular* prostitute and a *sacred* prostitute. Historically and prehistorically, at least in some European and Middle Eastern areas, there is considerable evidence that there were *sacred* female and male prostitutes providing sexual services sanctioned and sponsored within religious contexts (see references in Appendix A). When someone provided sexual services outside any religious sponsorship, they were called *secular* prostitutes.

In the modern Jewish, Christian, and Muslim world, many forms of sexual expression are forbidden or severely restricted religiously, legally, socially, with prostitution often being formally and violently oppressed (Mary Magdalene was about to be stoned when Jesus intervened). Except for a few safe havens in secret societies and unscrutinized indigenous cultures, today it is technically impossible to be a *sacred* prostitute, though one can in the modern world be of service sexually in a sacred way.

Whether sexual service is sacred or secular, however, is not really *the* question. This debate overlooks a basic premise of our religious, legal, and social culture: sex is innately sinful; and its corollary: the spirit is superior to the flesh.

As long as we hold these tenets—and most of us subconsciously do in some fashion—we can only begin to comprehend the profound contribution of women and men of the light to modern society.

A sexual-spiritual teacher/healer/initiator/catalyst knows sexuality as far more than technique and frictional stimulation. Sex is more than a coital position and the number of orgasms and "lasting longer" and gay, lesbian, bi, or straight. Sex is a dance of energy, a communion with ourselves, others, and Source. Sex is more than monogamy or open relationships or celibacy or virginity, for these simply are *forms* our sexual essence might take throughout a lifetime. Basically for these visionaries, we cannot not be sexual and we cannot not be spiritual—both are innately omnipresent within each of us.

Embracing this way of being in the world would greatly liberate our lives...the way we touch and communicate and experience pleasure and make love and sing our holy songs.

Sexuality and spirituality are far from antithetical; they are, in essence, One. This is the teaching, the wisdom, of the archetypal Mary Magdalene and women and men of the light. We must remember, though, they are only the messengers bearing a gift: the illuminated egg.

The choice to receive is ours...we have only to extend our open hand and open heart.

Appendix A

Resources for Becoming a Wo/Man of the Light

by

Kenneth Ray Stubbs, Editor

Women of the Light, the book, is written more to raise questions than to provide answers, for each person's reintegration of the sexual and the spiritual is a uniquely individual process.

To understand more or to become more like these women of the light, here are a few possible directions.

Numerous books and some videos can be very beneficial. The conceptual framework in *Women of the Light* relies extensively on Nancy Qualls-Corbett's *The Sacred Prostitute* and Merlin Stone's *When God Was a Woman*. Both are very highly recommended.

While much of the recent Goddess literature touches only lightly on the sacred prostitute, many of these books provide insightful information. Barbara G. Walker's *Woman's Encyclopedia of Myths and Secrets* is an essential resource. *The Once and Future Goddess* by Elinor W. Gadon is a clear and thoughtful presentation. Readers familiar with Jungian psychology may find Erich Neumann's *The Great Mother* a useful abstract analysis.

For a non-patriarchal perspective of Mary Magdalene, see Barbara G. Walker's *Woman's Encyclopedia of Myths and Secrets*, Nancy Qualls-Corbett's *The Sacred Prostitute*, and Elaine Pagels's *The Gnostic Gospels*.

Western sexology basically views sexuality as physical expression. For most women and men of the light as well as Tantric and shamanic followers, sexuality is mainly an energetic connection and flow. Alex Grey's visionary art in his *Sacred Mirrors* communicates this far better than most writings. Look here first if sex-as-energy is a foreign concept. My own *Sacred Orgasms* examines the energetic orgasm as a mystical experience. For a very valuable though extremely academic work on Chinese Taoist sexology (a tradition not discussed in *Women of the Light*), consult Douglas Wile's *Art of the Bedchamber*.

To explore sexuality in the shamanic world, read Bill Wahlberg's *Star Warrior: The Story of SwiftDeer*. This biography of Harley SwiftDeer, who was described in the FireWoman chapter, presents more on the Quodoushka spiritual sexuality tradition.

For more practical applications based on experiences from

wo/men of the light, try these writings from the contributors in this book: Betty Dodson's *Sex for One* and her video *Selfloving*; Carol Queen's *Exhibitionism for the Shy*; Jwala's *Sacred Sex*; and my *Sensual Ceremony*. For a self-help book based on sex surrogacy, see Adele Kennedy's *Touching for Pleasure*. Sex-positive massage can be learned from my *Erotic Massage* (book) and *Erotic Massage Video*. (Slightly different versions of these appear under the titles *Tantric Massage* and *Tantric Massage Video*.) Joseph Kramer's video *Fire on the Mountain: An Intimate Guide to Male Genital Massage* presents additional erotic massage techniques. Another useful resource for non-Western sexual energy approaches is *Sexual Energy Ecstasy* by David and Ellen Ramsdale.

Books and videos may be more accessible, but experiential live trainings go more to the core. If possible, study directly with the women of the light in this book. Their contact addresses follow in Appendix B.

For additional sacred-sex teachers, consult *Tantra: The Magazine* (from a local metaphysical bookstore or the publisher at P. O. Box 108, Torreon, NM 87061).

Sex surrogacy training information is available from the International Professional Surrogate Association (P. O. Box 74156, Los Angeles, CA 90004; telephone: (213) 469-4720).

To learn about training and volunteering on a sex information hot line, contact San Francisco Sex Information at (415) 621-7300. They are also available for answering any personal questions on sex.

Academic training in Western sexology is highly recommended from the Institute for the Advanced Study of Human Sexuality (1523 Franklin Street, San Francisco, CA 94109).

Unfortunately, sex-positive professional massage training is rare. Fine massage schools exist but none would not want to be listed here for fear of censure from an extremely sex-negative power structure in the massage profession.

Finding an ongoing sex-positive spiritual context is a difficult task. In the patriarchal Jewish, Christian, and Islamic religions, the women-are-inferior and sex-is-evil views are so strongly ingrained that little or no support for sexuality exploration, sacred or otherwise, can be found there. Even most gurus from the East are also sex-negative, suggesting that "lower" chakra meditation could lead one down the wrong path.

For me personally, I have often studied in established spiritual traditions focused on energy more than morality and then, on my own, integrated sexuality and energy teachings. Among the traditions I have found most beneficial are Tibetan Buddhism, Chinese Taoism (which is more of a philosophy than a religion), and some shamanic perspectives strongly influenced by Native American spirituality. Western Sufis (a branch of mystical Muslims) and followers of Bhagwan Shree Rajneesh, who shortly before his recent death became known as Osho, have often been keenly aware of sacred sexuality. Most Wiccan followers unfortunately have remained so underground that their earthy sexuality often goes unnoticed.

Though there is no room in most religious inns for sacred sexuality, incredible social and legal strides for sexual freedom have been made during the lifetime of the women of the light writing in this book. Still, we have so much farther to go. Anyone feeling drawn to the sacred sex light will have extensive opportunities to make a meaningful contribution to many men and women.

Fortunately, because there are few standardized professional regulations, each wo/man of the light can be fully creative, finding her or his own magical blend of satisfying self-expression. Equally important, *becoming* a wo/man of the light is a spiritual quest in itself.

Appendix B

Contacting the Writers

Arranged in alphabetical order by first name.

(addresses as of October 1994)

Betty Dodson

P. O. Box 1933
Murray Hill
New York, NY 10156

- To order *Selfloving: Video Portrait of a Women's Sexuality Seminar*, mail a $45.00 check made out to Betty Dodson. She will also send information on her new series of videos, workshops, and where to find her book, *Sex for One: The Joy of Selfloving*.

Carol Queen

Carol Queen Workshops
P. O. Box 471061
San Francisco, CA 94147-1061

- Offers workshops and classes and is available for public speaking. Her areas of expertise include sex and culture, sexual diversity, sexual enhancement and communication, erotic writing, and the sex industry. Write with S.A.S.E. for workshop listings, to request bibliography, or to contact regarding speaking engagements.

Carolyn Elderberry

P. O. Box 27266
Oakland, CA 94602

- Available for consultation, small groups, personal resource, or networking. "I would like to hear from those interested in Spirituality/Religion and Sex, and sex education."
- Send S.A.S.E. for sample newsletter.

Juliet Carr

P. O. Box 9463
Berkeley, CA 94709

- Send S.A.S.E. for information on individual consultations, workshops, books, videos, stage shows, and availability for seminars and speaking engagements.

Jwala

Kathleen Bingham
775 E. Blithedale, # 174
Mill Valley, CA 94941
Voice Mail: (415) 995-4643

- To order her book *Sacred Sex: Ecstatic Techniques for Empowering Relationships*, mail a $19.95 check or money order (CA residents: $21.25, including sales tax) made out to Kathleen Bingham.

- Write for current information on Sacred Sex seminars, Sluts and Goddesses events, Breath Orgasm classes, as well as audio and video tapes.

Kenneth Ray Stubbs

P. O. Box 67-WI
Larkspur, CA 94977-0067

- Write for information on books and videos: *Erotic Massage* (with accompanying video), *Romantic Interludes, The Clitoral Kiss, Tantric Massage* (with accompanying video), *Sensual Ceremony,* and *Sacred Ceremony.*
- Note: Seminars and individual sessions are no longer available.

Shell Freye

Couples' swinging house parties held in Oakland, California, on Saturday nights only. Couples, please call together for information: (510) 834-5808

- Shell Freye, Clinical Sexologist, is available for private sessions on sexual dysfunctions as well as sexual and sensual enhancement. Contact at telephone above.

Stephanie Rainbow Lightning Elk

Stephanie Wadell
P. O. Box 60971
Palo Alto, CA 94306

- Stephanie Wadell is a sexuality consultant specializing in spiritual sexuality disciplines, sex therapy, and sensuality enhancement. Write for information on Quodoushka seminars and ceremonies, as well as private consultations concerning spiritual sexuality.

NOTE: **Richard Stodart**, the artist of the front-cover Mary Magdalene painting, can be reached at Rte. 3, Box 142, Burgess, VA 22432.

ACKNOWLEDGMENTS

by

Kenneth Ray Stubbs, Editor

First and foremost, I wish to express my deep appreciation to the women of the light who wrote for this book. For several, writing down their personal story was a new challenge. For many, being publicly associated with the controversial topic of sacred *prostitute* was not always a comfortable position. Collectively they have told the story that for many years I have known could be honorably told.

My editorial role has been greatly eased by the "editorial support team": Chyrelle D. Chasen, Karen Crane, Pam Johnson, Nancy Carleton, and Clara Kerns. I am deeply grateful to them. Several other friends have given valuable feedback along the way: Laurie Immoos, Carole Merette, Richard Stodart, Penny Hancock, C. Jeanine Stephens, Chris McMahon, Eurydice Feibusch, and Stan Lipkin. Much thanks to Carol Heller for her assistance in writing the Group-Sex Hostess chapter. A special thanks to Marcia Singer. And Sandy Trupp, as always, has been supportive in so many ways.

For the cover of this book, Richard Stodart painted Mary Magdalene far more profoundly than I had hoped for. His mystical wisdom and artistic ability continue to nurture me.

Were it not for the special women and men of the light who have graced my life, the seed for this book would never have come to fruition. I thank you and celebrate your gifts.

Index

Other Books by the Contributing Writers

By Betty Dodson

Sex for One: The Joy of Selfloving

By Carol Queen

Exhibitionism for the Shy: Show Off, Dress Up, and Talk Hot

By Jwala

Sacred Sex: Ecstatic Techniques for Empowering Relationships

By Kenneth Ray Stubbs

Tantric Massage: An Illustrated Manual for Meditative Sexuality
Sacred Orgasms: Teachings From the Heart
Sensual Ceremony: A Contemporary Tantric Guide to Sexual Intimacy
Erotic Massage: The Touch of Love
Romantic Interludes: A Sensuous Lovers Guide
*The Clitoral Kiss: A Fun Guide to Oral Sex, Oral Massage, and Other
        Oral Delights*